To Rena
Pray Psalms for
Pray Godliness
Elmer Towns

PRAYING

—the—

PSALMS

ELMER L. TOWNS

PRAYING
—the—
PSALMS

To Touch God and Be Touched by Him

Destiny Image® Publishers, Inc.
P.O. Box 310
Shippensburg, PA 17257-0310

*"Speaking to the Purposes of God for This Generation
and for the Generations to Come"*

ISBN 0-7684-2195-0

For Worldwide Distribution
Printed in the U.S.A.

This book and all other Destiny Image, Revival Press, MercyPlace,
Fresh Bread, Destiny Image Fiction, and Treasure House books are
available at Christian bookstores and distributors worldwide.

2 3 4 5 6 7 8 9 10 / 10 09 08 07 06

For a U.S. bookstore nearest you, call
1-800-722-6774.

For more information on foreign distributors, call
717-532-3040.

Or reach us on the Internet:
www.destinyimage.com

ENDORSEMENTS

My wife and I began praying each of the Psalms, and when we got to Psalm 2 the entire reading opened up to us. We had never seen the Lord Jesus Christ in that Psalm. We shared *Praying the Psalms* with a godly pastor who said, "This is magnificent!" I would beg you to pray the Psalms daily, because it will take your worship to a higher level.

Doug Oldham, Gospel Singer
Three gold and one platinum record awards
Gospel Singer of the Year, 1974

Praying the Psalms is a wonderful way to meet God every day in your private devotions. You cannot get closer to God than when you pray the Scriptures. Since the Book of Psalms reflects the heart of God, you will get close to His heart when you pray the Psalms.

Bill Bright

TABLE OF CONTENTS

HOW TO PRAY

INTRODUCTION

Lord, I love to pray the Psalms because they express my passion, and I feel deeply when I read them. The Psalmist was pouring out his soul to You about the things that deeply moved him. Lord, I join him in prayer. The Psalmist journeyed into Your heart, O Lord, and that is where I want to go. I want to pray the Psalms, and look into Your heart.

Lord, I want to cry when the Psalmist weeps, shout when the Psalmist rejoices, burn when the Psalmist gets angry, and fall on my face when the Psalmist worships You.

This book is a modern day translation of the Psalms into prayers so you can identify with and pray them. But not all the Psalms were originally prayers to God. Some Psalms were originally written as devotional thoughts about God (Psalm 23); a few Psalms pour out anger at enemies (Psalms 3 and 4). Some Psalms are instructional (Psalm 119), teaching the law of God. But I have transposed all of them into prayers in modern language so you can use the words of the Psalms to talk to God.

Lord, I want You to feel my passionate love for You as I pray these Psalms, and I want You to feel my anger as I vent my feelings about evil people. Sometimes I pray these Psalms begging You for protection . . . for rest . . . or from relief from pain. Sometimes I intercede to You for forgiveness, or for Your guidance in my life. I need to touch You and let You touch me. I pray these Psalms to enter Your presence.

I know the Bible is God's Word—every word—that's what I teach. So why did I update Bible words and add some modern terms and phrases? I did it to help you the reader understand the Psalms and pray them daily. Isn't that why God gave you the Psalms—so you would pray to Him and help you live for Him? So with all reverence for the original Hebrew version of Psalms, I've tried to apply them to modern language so you can pray the Psalms passionately. Don't let this version of Psalms substitute for the original; read the Scriptures constantly. Read all of them reverently, because then you are holding God's Word in your hands.

Lord, I love Your Word the Scriptures. Help me love You better as I study the Psalms. Help the prayers of this book open my eyes to see You more clearly, and find deeper insight into the Word of God.

This book is just a tool for *Praying the Psalms*. If it contributes to your life, give God the praise. For any good insight, I give credit to my Hebrew professors in seminary and the research tools I've used. For any weaknesses, I take full responsibility.

Lord, overlook the weaknesses of this book and help readers effectively pray the Psalms. Don't let them get hung up on phrases or differences in words. Help them see the meaning behind the words of Scripture Psalms and pray the Psalms to You. Lord, help intercessors prevail with Psalms of intercession . . . help worshippers adore You with Psalms of worship . . . help beginners feel Your presence by their first attempts at prayer.

May you the reader touch God through these Psalms, and in return, may God touch you.

Elmer Towns
From my home at the foot of the
Blue Ridge Mountains of Virginia
Winter, A.D. 2002

WHAT ARE THE PSALMS?

This may be the first portion of Scripture that you've read seriously. So you ask, "What is a Psalm?" The Psalms were written as prayers for the Hebrew people to sing. The song was their deep feeling *about God,* or as a prayer *to God.* In Bible times as you passed a field you might have heard the workers singing one of the Psalms. Or you might have heard a family singing a Psalm as they relaxed in the evening sitting under their fig tree. *Lord, I sing my passion to You.*

Each Psalm is a worship event. Therefore, I've rewritten some of the Psalms, that describe God, into prayers. Instead of reading, "The Lord is my shepherd," you'll pray, "Lord, You are my shepherd." Now, each Psalm is a prayer to God. *Lord, teach me to talk to You.*

The Psalms are a mirror that reflects your soul. As you pray them, you'll see in these mirrors your sin and hypocrisy more clearly than ever before. So pray the Psalms of repentance and turn to God. But you'll also see in these mirrors the essence of a godly life. Then pray with the Psalmist, "As the young deer being chased will thirst for water, so my soul longs for Your presence, O God" (Ps. 42:1, PTP). Look deep into each mirror and you'll see God. While this is not a theology textbook on God, you'll see many facets of His person and attributes as you are *Praying the Psalms. Lord, I want to know You.*

The Psalms are poetry, not like English poetry, i.e., "Roses are red, violets are blue, the angles in Heaven know I surely love you." Hebrew poetry had neither rhyme nor meter. Their poetry had rhythm; as they accentuated different phrases, so that the content of phrases matched. Did you get what I just said, i.e., *content?* The secret of Hebrew poetry is matching thoughts, not matching rhymes or meter. The Hebrews matched their phrases in four ways.

Synonymous poetry is when the thought in the first phrase is repeated in the second phrase. "Hear this, all peoples; give ear, all inhabitants of the world" (Ps. 49:1).

Antithetic poetry is when the thought of the first phrase is the opposite of the idea in the second line. "The wicked borrows and does not repay, but the righteous shows mercy and gives" (Ps. 37:21).

In *synthetic poetry* the idea in the first phrase is the basis for a statement in the second line, and completes it. "The law of the Lord is perfect, converting the soul; the testimony of the Lord is sure, making wise the simple" (Ps. 19:7).

In *climactic poetry* the idea in the first line is incomplete but builds to a conclusion in the second line, or sometimes the third line. "Blessed is the man who walks not in the counsel of the ungodly, nor stands in the path of sinners, nor sits in the seat of the scornful" (Ps. 1:1).

When reading the Psalms in Scripture, there is a title with explanations before many Psalms (but not all Psalms). In this volume the titles are included as a footnote. Some scholars treat them as inspired text, some do not. In the inscriptions, the word *shiggalon* has been changed to "A Psalm of praise." The word *maschil* is changed to "A Psalm of instruction." The word *michtan* is changed to "A Psalm carved in stone," because the word means "to carve" or "to place on a monument." *Lord, I want my heart to sing these prayers to You.*

PRAYER GUIDE TO THE PSALMS

Where To Look When You Have A Need To Pray

When you are *grateful*	1, 70, 81, 106, 116, 118, 124, 127, 145
When you are *thankful*	1, 8, 18, 30, 37, 45, 48, 53, 59, 63, 65, 66, 78, 81, 87, 89, 98, 100, 104, 105, 106, 111
Imprecatory prayers	2, 3, 4, 5, 7, 9, 10, 11, 12, 17, 21, 44, 52, 54, 55, 58, 69, 74, 75, 79, 83, 109, 110, 129, 140
A prayer when you face an *enemy*	3, 4, 5, 7, 9, 10, 11, 12, 13, 17, 18, 20, 21, 22, 24, 31, 34, 35, 36, 37, 44, 51, 54, 55, 56, 57
A prayer for God to *listen* to you	6, 28, 35, 69, 71, 77, 123
A prayer about *creation*	8, 19, 28, 93, 94, 103, 104
A prayer for *protection* from danger	13, 17, 18, 20, 21, 22, 23, 24, 25, 27, 28, 31, 34, 35, 37, 40, 44, 46, 56, 57, 58, 60, 62
Those who deny God	14
A prayer for *assurance*	15, 20, 26

A prayer when facing *death*	49, 50, 90, 91
A prayer about the resurrection and *Kingdom*	16, 46, 49, 50, 67, 72, 76, 82, 83, 85, 89, 90, 97, 132
A prayer for *wisdom*	19, 126
A prayer for *guidance*	23, 25, 39, 40, 126
A prayer for *intimacy* with God	27, 42, 46, 84, 131
When you desire to be in God's *sanctuary*	27, 84
A prayer for God to *reveal* Himself to you	29, 42, 131
A prayer for *forgiveness*	32, 51, 66, 80, 85, 88, 107, 130
A prayer to *bless others*	33, 36, 137
A prayer when *suffering*	38, 41
A prayer for *healing*	41
A prayer for hope when you are *discouraged*	43, 102
A prayer for those in *authority* over you	45, 61
A prayer to *glorify God*	47, 57, 63, 73, 76, 93, 95, 96, 98, 104, 113, 128, 134, 146, 147, 148, 149, 150
A prayer about *Jerusalem*	48, 65, 84, 87, 89, 122, 126
A prayer to receive *God's blessing*	49, 65, 90, 92, 101, 115, 120, 123, 125, 126, 127, 133, 147

A prayer for *restoration*	51, 80, 102, 107, 116, 130, 137
A prayer of *rejoicing*	63, 97, 100, 115
A prayer of thanksgiving for God's *sovereignty*	99, 105, 106, 111, 113, 114, 118, 121, 136, 139, 145, 146, 147, 148
A prayer for *the Word of God*	19, 119, 135
A prayer of *thanksgiving*	112, 113, 116, 135, 139, 145, 148, 149, 150
A prayer when you are facing an *enemy*	58, 59, 60, 61, 62, 64, 68, 69, 75, 86, 91, 94, 95, 108, 120, 138, 141, 142, 143, 144

GETTING READY
TO PRAY THE PSALMS

Prayer is not difficult, it is simply *talking to God.* I do it, you can do it, everyone does it. You can talk to God. This book is prepared to help you talk to God. *Lord, I want to talk to You.*

The word *Psalm* in Hebrew is *Tehillum,* which means, "to make jubilant music." So this book is actually prayers that are prayed to music. When the Psalms were translated, they were given the Greek title *Psalmo,* which means "songs." The title was brought over into English, so today we call them *Psalms.* The Hebrew *Tehillum* is from a root *halal,* "to rejoice," or to "yell a greeting." It's the word from which we get the word *hello.* So, when you're praying the *halal,* happily greet the Lord of the universe. *Hello God, this is me, thank You for listening to me.*

There are many ways we talk to people. We ask for things . . . we thank them . . . we informally chat . . . we negotiate . . . we express anger . . . we complain . . . and we compliment. Likewise, there are many ways to pray. As you pray the various Psalms, notice all the different ways you talk to God. *Lord, teach me to pray every possible way.*

The first way to talk to God is by complimenting Him. This is called worship in Scripture. "Come, let us worship and bow down; let us kneel before the Lord our Maker" (Ps. 95:6). You worship by giving the "worth" to God that is due Him. You worship God by giving Him worthship. Since He is due all worship, we should not worship self, false gods, or worldly pleasures. *Lord, I worship Your majesty.*

Jesus taught us, "True worshippers will worship the Father in spirit and truth: for the Father is seeking people to worship Him this way" (Jn. 4:23, author's translation). To worship God in *spirit* is to pour over our entire spirit to Him in praise, not holding anything back. To worship the Father in *truth* is to follow the way God taught us in the Word of God, also called the Word of truth. *Lord, I worship You with my whole heart, and I worship You the way the Bible (truth) tells me to do it.*

The second way to pray *is* to ask for forgiveness. You can't pray when sin blocks your access to God. The Psalmist notes, "If I regard iniquity in my heart, the Lord will not hear" (Ps. 66:18). So you pray the Psalms to ask for forgiveness, "According to the multitude of Your tender mercies, blot out my transgressions" (Ps. 51:1). Then you can rejoice with the Psalmist because God "forgives all your iniquities" (Ps. 103:3). You ought to know, "There is forgiveness with You [God], that You may be feared" (Ps. 130:4). You ought to worship and thank God for forgiving your sins. *Lord, thank You for forgiving all my past . . . present . . . and future sins.*

A third way you pray *is* by yielding yourself to God. It's called surrendering to Him. The Lord's Prayer tells you to pray like this, "Thy will be done." You became a follower of the Lord by yielding to Him. Now each day you ought to renew that decision. *Lord, today I give myself to You.*

Psalm 100 gives us a picture of people presenting themselves to God. "We are His people and the sheep of His pasture" (v. 3). As you follow the Lord, you "enter into His gates with thanksgiving" (v. 4), which means you bring a thank offering to God. Then you enter "His courts with praise" (v. 4). *Lord, today I again present my body a living sacrifice. I yield to Your will.*

A fourth way to pray *is* to ask protection. What scares you today? Is it bankruptcy? Loss of family? Disease? Terrorist attacks? Physical disability? God can protect you from fear and dread. You may have a disease and will die, but God can give you victory of spirit, so that death becomes the gift of God. Or, God may give you the gift of healing. The Psalmist prayed, "This poor man cried out, and the Lord heard him, and saved him out of all his troubles" (Ps. 34:6). Notice the word *troubles* is plural. God delivered him from all kinds of troubles. How many kinds of troubles are you in today? Then the Psalmist tells us in the next verse how the Lord will deliver you. "The angel of the Lord encamps all around those who fear Him, and delivers them" (Ps. 34:7). *Lord, deliver me from the dangers I face, and the dangers I don't know about.*

A fifth way to pray *is* to ask for guidance. Are you searching for an answer to a decision or problem today? If so, *Praying the Psalms* can help you find it. You can find God's will for your life in prayer. God promises, "I will guide you" (Ps. 32:8). And based on that promise you can have assurance that He will lead you. "He leads me" (Ps. 23:2). *Lord, take me by the hand and guide me through my difficult decisions.*

A sixth way to pray *is* to ask for His victory. All God's people want to overcome sin (Ps. 51) or conquer an enemy (Ps. 7). The Psalmist promises victory today, in the strength of the Lord, "Through God we will do valiantly, for it is He who shall tread down our enemies" (Ps. 60:12). The

Psalmist also promises future victory, "I will dwell in the house of the Lord forever" (Ps. 23:6). *Lord, I want victory now, I'm tired of being defeated, I want victory today.*

A seventh prayer *is* for provision. You ask other people for things, why not ask God? The Psalmist wanted the blessing of God that included good crops, flourishing flocks, healthy families, and good health. However, the Old Testament saint did not ask for things, and money, and answers to prayer as they are taught in the New Testament. In the Old Testament Psalms, it seems the Psalmist felt if he trusted God, obeyed God, and worked hard, God would bless him with material things. "The Lord has been mindful of us; He will bless us; He will bless the house of Israel; He will bless the house of Aaron. He will bless those who fear the Lord, both small and great. May the Lord give you increase more and more, you and your children" (Ps. 115:12-14). Asking is the kingdom principle taught by Jesus. He said, "Up to now you have not asked for anything in prayer, now you will receive when you ask in My name" (Jn. 16:24, author's translation). *Lord, I have many needs; teach me to ask properly for my daily bread.*

Praying for blessing on your service to God is the eighth way to pray. Moses prayed for victory in battle, while Joshua led the army into battle (Ex. 17:8-16). When Moses was physically unable to continue holding up his arms in prayer, Aaron and Hur helped him. David prayed, "O Lord, when I cry ... have mercy also upon me, and answer me" (Ps. 27:7). The Psalmist confesses, "I would have lost heart, unless I had believed that I would see the goodness of the Lord in the land of the living" (Ps. 27:13). *Lord, I want to see Your hand in my service for You.*

Practicing Prayer

Prayer is the most universally common utterance of people. People around the world don't pray the same way ... to the same god ... for the same reason ... nor do they *base* the answer to their prayer on the same principles. *But* people around the world pray. However, there's only one way to pray, because there is only one true God in this world, while there are many false gods. If you want your prayers answered, you must come God's way. Elijah prayed on Mt. Carmel, "Lord God of Abraham, Isaac, and Israel, let it be known this day that You are God in Israel and I am Your servant, and that I have done all these things at Your word. Hear me, O Lord" (1 Kings 18:36-37). *Lord, I believe you're the only God and I believe You answer prayer.*

1. *Pray sincerely.* You must pray the words of Elijah, as sincerely as Elijah prayed. You must sincerely believe because, "He who comes

to God must believe that He is, and that He is a rewarder of those who diligently seek Him" (Heb. 11:6).

2. *Pray passionately.* As you pray the words of the Psalmists in 21st-century language, you must get into their skin. You must feel their passion. You must come to God the way they come to God. Your request can become just as important as their requests, if you pray with all your heart. *Lord, I believe in You, help my unbelief* (Mk. 9:24).

3. *One prayer at a time.* Don't try to see how fast you can read through these Psalms. Pray it once, then think about what you've prayed, Selah! Then pray the Psalm again.

4. *Compare with Scripture.* Either before or after you've prayed a prayer in this book, read it in Scripture. Remember *Praying the Psalms* is not a translation, so don't look for word by word similarity. Look for the same meaning. When you pray the Psalms in modern language, God should hear the same message from you as He heard from the original Psalmist who prayed the Psalm.

   When you read Scripture, you first interpret the meaning of the verse from the words. Then you apply the Scripture to life. As you enter into *Praying the Psalms*, you should arrive at the correct interpretation and meaning of the Psalm.

5. *Write down your prayer experiences.* I began writing my prayer requests in 1951 and I still have those sheets of paper from those early years. Why? Because those prayer requests continue to teach me how to pray. I've learned why God didn't answer, and on occasion I've experienced miraculous answers to prayer.

   You should write down your requests, then keep a written copy when answers come. Also, you'll want to write the lessons that God is teaching you as you pray.

6. *Pray one Psalm each day.* Your goal is not speed, but depth. Pray one prayer each day and determine not to go to the next until you've learned what God is teaching you. However, some prayers are long; it might take two or three days to learn everything from some of the lengthy Psalms. When I was writing this book, I set a goal to write one Psalm a day. Obviously, I couldn't keep up with that schedule, writing and prayer, plus everything else I had to do. Even though my study and writing became part of my daily devotions, some Psalms took a week to write.

Obviously, it took much longer for the longest chapter in the Bible, i.e., Psalm 119.

7. *Bring an open heart.* When you come to God, don't try to tell Him what to do, or how to answer your prayers. As you enter into *Praying the Psalms*, let the Lord speak to you and lead you. Remember, you're not reading a prayer, you're talking to God.

May God bless you as you daily *Pray the Psalms.*
Elmer Towns

PSALM 1

*A Prayer Of Gratitude For God's Blessing**

I am happily blessed, O Lord, so I don't:

 Walk according to ungodly counsel,

 Hang out with sinners,

 Sit with scorners.

Lord, I delight to live by Your principles,

 And I love to meditate in Your Word.

Lord, may I be like a hearty tree

 Planted by living waters;

That each season bears spiritual fruit,

 Whose leaf never stops growing.

The ungodly are not so:

 They are like the husk the wind blows away,

 They shall be punished in Your judgment,

 They shall not enter the congregation of Your people.

Lord, You watch over the path of those who do right;

 But the path of the ungodly leads to destruction.

Amen

*A Psalm describing two types of people.

PSALM 2

*A Prayer To God About Those Who Rebel Against Him And His Son**

Lord, I don't understand why the unsaved rage
    And fight against Your plans.
Why rulers do everything contrary to Your will,
    And resist the ways of Christ.
They strive to throw off Your restraints,
    And say, "Let us get rid of these chains."

But You Lord, laugh as You sit in Heaven;
    And You scoff at their rebellion.
You are angry at their defiance,
    Terrifying them with Your judgment.
You have declared, "I established My King to rule;
    He will reign from the holy hill of Zion."

Your king is Your only begotten Son,
    He will execute Your will on earth.
You have given Him all people and ethnic groups,
    He owns the uttermost parts of the earth.

Your Son will punish rebellion with a rod of iron,
    He shall crush rebels in their defiance.
What should be the response of the kings of the earth,
    And what should human judges do?

Tremble before the Son because He is the Lord,
    Serve Him with fear.
Love the Son, lest He be angry;

When He destroys all rebellion that stands in His way.
Blessed are all those who trust Your Son.

Amen

*A Psalm of the rejected king.

HOW TO PRAY

When You Need To Pause And Meditate: Selah

The word *Selah* comes from two roots, i.e., *Salah,* which means, "to praise," and *Salai,* which means, "to lift up." Therefore, you don't have to guess that this word means "to lift up God in praise." *Lord, I will lift You up in my prayers.*

However, some think the word *Selah* is a musical note. But when examined carefully, it deals with the subject matter of the Psalms, not its musical expression. It deals with truth, not tunes.

Sometimes the word *Selah* occurs at the beginning of a phrase, at other times at the end, and sometimes it comes in the middle of a verse. What does this mean? We know that it does not end a verse, nor does it begin a phrase. Rather, it *connects* two thoughts or phrases together. Therefore, *Selah is a thought link.* When you see the word *Selah,* look back at what has been said as a basis to praise God. Then mark that thought, and connect it with the thought that follows. *Lord, because You have answered my prayers in the past, Selah, I will pray again.*

Some think the word means "to pause." It may be that, *but* it is not a pause for the instruments of music. Rather it is a pause for the singer to think about what he has been singing. That way the singer can understand it and connect it with what is going to be sung.

Some have said the word *Selah* is "to lift up," therefore, it means to sing louder. Today in piano we use the term *crescendo.* But it is not the music that becomes louder. Our hearts are to be lifted up in worship and praise to God for the truth that connects to our life.

The word *Selah* occurs seventy-four times in the Old Testament. Seventy-one times are found in the Book of Psalms. It occurs first in Psalm 3:2. It is found three times in the prayer of Habakkuk (chapter 3).

Several early Christian writers (e.g., St. Jerome) suggested that the word *Selah* should be translated "forever." However, there is no support for this. Other Christians compared it to the "Amen" that was said by Christians or sung by Christians in their hymns.

When you see the word *Selah* in the Psalms, stop and meditate, which is another way of saying, "Stop and think about what you have just prayed." Therefore, it is possible that you could pray, *Lord, answer my prayer, Selah.*

PSALM 3

*A Prayer For God To Defeat Your Enemies**

Lord, I have many enemies
  That are trying to destroy me.
They tell me not to look to You,
  Because there is no help in God. Selah!

But You, Lord, are my protecting shield;
  You lift me up with encouragement.
I cried out to You for help,
  You answered me from Your holy mountain. Selah!

I was able to lie down and sleep,
  Because You protected me during the night.
Now I am not afraid of ten thousand enemies,
  Because You are on every side to protect me.

Smite my enemy on his head,
  Shut the mouth of those who criticize me;
Deliverance comes from You, O Lord;
  Bless Your people with victory. Selah!

Amen

*A Psalm of David, when he fled from Absalom his son.

PSALM 4

*A Prayer About Your Enemies When Thoughts About Them Keep You From Sleep**

Lord, answer my prayer;
  You know I am sincere.
I am concerned and distressed,
  Because You have not answered my prayers.
People are accusing me of many things,
  They are attempting to ruin my reputation;
  How long will they attack me? Selah!

Lord, I am certain of one thing;
  You have set apart the godly for Yourself,
  You will listen to me when I call.
I will not give in to the sin of anger,
  But will think about You as I go to sleep.
I will confess my sin and get forgiveness,
  Because You are my Lord.

Many tell me there are better ways to find a good time,
  But the enjoyment of Your presence gives me more
  satisfaction than food and money has given to them.
Lord, I will lie down and sleep in peace;
  Because I know I am safe in You. Selah!

                                        Amen

*A Psalm of David.

PSALM 5

*A Prayer Of Commitment To God And A Request To Eliminate Enemies**

O Lord, listen to my words;
  Consider the things I am thinking.
O my God and my King, listen to my prayers;
  Because I am speaking to You.
I know You will hear me in the morning,
  Because it is then that I look to You and pray.

I know You do not get pleasure out of wickedness,
  Nor is evil found in You.
Those who sin foolishly cannot enter Your presence,
  Because You hate the iniquity they do.

You will destroy those who blaspheme,
  Because You reject murderers and liars.
But I can come into Your presence,
  Because in mercy You receive me.

I fear Your punishment,
  Therefore, I worship You in Your holy temple.
Lord, help me always do the right thing,
  Especially as I deal with my enemies;
  I want to live blameless before Your face.

Lord, I know my enemies never speak of Your faithfulness;
  They inwardly desire wickedness,
  Their throat is a grave,
  So, I cannot trust their words.

Destroy them, O Lord, with the same damnation
    That they plan for others,
    Because they constantly break Your law,
    And they continually rebel against You.

Lord, because I have put my trust in You,
    And because You destroy my enemies,
    I constantly shout for joy.

Let everyone that loves You, O Lord,
    Constantly rejoice in You.
I know You will bless the righteous, O Lord,
    You will constantly defend them.

Amen

*A Psalm of David.

PSALM 6

*A Prayer For God To Listen And Answer**

Lord, don't fuss at me because You are angry at my failures;
    Don't punish me because I've not pleased You.
Have mercy on my weakness, O Lord;
    Heal me because I am crushed.

Lord, I am disappointed in my failures,
    How long will I have to put up with my weaknesses?
Come deliver me, Lord, from human frailties,
    Because You are merciful, I need You to save me from myself.

If I die, how can I serve You on earth?
    How can I worship You in the grave?

I'm sick and tired of feeling bad about my failures,

    I go to bed crying over my sin,

    All night long I weep over my predicament.

My eyes are red because I can't cry any longer,

    Grief has made an old man out of me.

I want everyone who accuses me of sin to leave me alone,

    You, Lord, have listened to my repentance;

You have heard my prayers,

    You will answer my request.

Lord, make my enemies ashamed of their accusations;

    Punish them quickly for their complaints.

                         Amen

*A Psalm of David.

PSALM 7

*A Prayer For God To Punish The Wicked**

O Lord, I trust You with my life;

    Save me from those who persecute me.

They want to rip me in pieces like a lion,

    Thinking no one will deliver me.

O Lord, let my enemies persecute me if I deserve it;

    If my hands have sinned,

        If I have attacked those at peace with me,

    (Actually, I've done good to my enemies).

O Lord, if I have done evil things;

    Let my enemies stomp me under foot,

Let them drag my honor through the dirt. Selah!
O Lord, wake up Your righteous anger;
    Because my enemies are attacking me.
    Awaken to carry out Your judgment.

O Lord, let Your people gather about You;
    Return so they can enjoy Your presence.

O Lord, I know You will judge all people;
    Judge me first and see that I try to do right.
    Examine me to see my integrity.

O Lord, stop the wicked from doing wickedness,
    Let the righteous do righteously.
You can do this because You know the hearts of all;
    Therefore, You are angry with the wicked.
    And You are pleased with the righteous.

If the wicked will not repent,
    You will bring the sword of war against them,
    You will attack them with the arrows of persecution,
    You will visit them with death.

My enemy is a friend of iniquity,
    He thinks constantly of harming others.
He always is digging a trap,
    But he falls into his self-made destruction.

His attack on others ends up hurting himself,
    His wounds are self-inflicted.
But You, O Lord, will I praise;

For You always deal with everyone rightly,

I will praise Your name, O Lord, Most High.

Amen

*A Psalm of praise by David, which he sang unto the Lord, concerning the words of Cush the Benjamite.

PSALM 8

*A Prayer Of Thanksgiving For Your Place In Creation**

O Lord, Your name is the most excellent one on earth;

You have glorified Yourself by creating Heaven.

You are praised by babies and infants,

But You will not accept praise by Your enemies.

When I look at the heavens, I see the work of Your fingers;

You planned the moon and the stars.

Then I realize mankind is so insignificant,

But You reveal Yourself to us who are just humans.

You made us lower than the angels,

And you crown us with glory and honor.

You gave us rule over Your creation,

You put it under our control.

You have given us sheep, oxen, and other animals;

This includes birds, fish, and sea creatures.

O Lord, You are our Lord;

How excellent is Your name on earth.

Amen

*A Psalm of David.

PSALM 9

*A Prayer For Deliverance From Your Enemies And For God To Punish Them**

Lord, I praise You with my whole heart;
   I tell everyone about Your marvelous works.
Lord, I sing praises to Your name most high;
   I'm happy when I rejoice in You.

When my enemies return to attack me,
   They will fail because Your presence is with me.
You support me because I live by the right principles,
   You always support the right thing.
You rebuke the unsaved who act wickedly,
   Let no one remember them.
Lord, destroy my enemies;
   Destroy their cities and any memory of them.

But You, Lord, will continue forever;
   You sit upon Your throne to judge all people.
You judge every one in the right way,
   You judge every one by the right standards.
O Lord, those who are oppressed want to hide in You;
   They want You to be their refuge in troubled times.
You have not forsaken those who put You first,
   Because they put their trust in You.

I sing praises to You in Zion,
   I will tell all people of Your works.
You do not forget to punish murderers,
   Nor do You forget the plea of the humble.

Lord, be merciful to me when my enemies attack me;
    Don't let them kill me.
I want those near You in the temple to hear me praise You.
    I rejoice in Your salvation.

The unsaved fall into the evil trap they set for their enemies,
    They are imprisoned in the cell they prepare for others.
Lord, You are known by the right ways You judge people;
    The wicked are condemned to the punishment they plan for others.
    Selah!
You turn the wicked into the anguish of punishment,
    You also put the people who deny You into hell.

You will not overlook the needy,
    You will also watch over the poor.
Come down, O Lord, so that the wicked will not have their way;
    Bring them before You to be judged.
Make the heathen fear You and Your judgment,
    So they will be accountable to You like everyone else. Selah!

                                              Amen

*A Psalm of David.

PSALM 10

A Prayer For The Punishment Of The Wicked

Lord, why are You so far away from me;
    When I need You most, You seem to hide?
The wicked intentionally hurt those who can't defend themselves.
    I pray they suffer the same pain they plan for others.
These wicked boast about their tricks,
    They stick up for other evil people, but hate You, O Lord.

The wicked are too proud to seek You,
  They never realize they will have to answer to You.

Because every evil thing they do succeeds,
  They laugh at their victims;
  They don't know You will punish them someday.
The wicked boast, "I'm not going to get hurt,
  I am free to do anything I want."

Lord, the mouth of the wicked is full of cursing and lies;
  Their evil plans are on the tip of their tongue.
They crouch like a lion in dark shadows
  Waiting to pounce on defenseless victims.
Like a hungry lion goes searching for food,
  They go looking for their next helpless prey.
Then the wicked drag their bodies away,
  Because the weak can't defend themselves.

The wicked say, "God is not watching,
  He doesn't know what I do, He doesn't care!"
Come down, O Lord, punish the wicked;
  Do not forget those who can't defend themselves.
The wicked think they can get away with their treachery,
  They think You will never punish them.
But You have seen every thing the wicked have done,
  You will not forget those who can't defend themselves.
You remember every thought and act of every wicked person.
  You will take care of those who can't take care of themselves.

Break the arm of the wicked,
  Don't let any of them get away,
Lord, You are our King who lives forever;

Get rid of those who worship false gods.

Lord, You understand the desires of those who can't help themselves.

Hear their prayers for deliverance.

Bring justice to the helpless of this world,

So they can live in peace.

Amen

PSALM 11

*A Prayer For God's Judgment On Those Who Attack His Truth**

I trust You, Lord, when trouble comes;

Even though people tell me to hide in the mountains.

They tell me to fly away like a bird.

My enemies are getting ready to attack me,

They have bow and arrows to kill me,

They will attack any one who lives right.

Lord, if Your foundations of truth are destroyed;

What can we do who live by Your principles?

Lord, I recognize You are in Your holy temple;

You see everything from Your throne in Heaven,

You will judge all people by what You see.

Lord, examine both those who live right;

And those who hate Your principles.

Lord, punish those who rebel against You

With the fire and brimstone of hell.
Give them what they deserve.

Because You are a righteous God,
    You love those who do right.
    You favor them with Your presence.
                                Amen

*A Psalm of David.

PSALM 12

A Prayer Against The Enemy's Propaganda

Lord, help me to be godly;
    There are so few left who are faithful.
The ones I expect to follow You
    They are falling away.

They talk with their friends about fleshly things,
    They lie about You and the truth;
    Telling others it's alright not to follow You.

Lord, one day You will shut them up,
    They won't be able to lie about You any more.
They won't be able to justify their sin,
    They won't be able to say anything they desire;
    They won't be able to deny Your rule over them.

Lord, come strengthen the weak who are resisting
the enemy's arguments;
    Your followers are being knocked down,
    They are gasping for spiritual breath.

Lord, I know Your words are better than what the enemy says;

    I have repeatedly tried Your promises and they never fail.

Lord, I know You will keep those who trust in Your Word;

    You will preserve them from the enemy's lies,

    Even when the enemy is all about them.

Amen

*A Psalm of David.

PSALM 13

*A Prayer For Perseverance Against The Enemy's Attacks**

Lord, it seems like You have forgotten me;

    How long will You hide Your face when I need You?

Lord, I keep looking for You inside my heart;

    But all I see are shadows and bitterness

    Because my enemies are defeating me.

Hear me, O Lord, I need Your help;

    Show me what to do or I'll die.

I don't want my enemies to gloat over me,

    Thinking they have made me surrender.

Lord, I trust in Your mercy to save me;

    I know You will deliver me.

Then, I will worship You with singing;

    Because You will abundantly bless me.

Amen

*A Psalm of David.

PSALM 14

*A Prayer About Those Who Deny God**

Lord, fools say You do not exist.

> They deny You to justify their corrupt lifestyle.
>
> They deny You because they don't want to do good.

Lord, look down from Heaven into the hearts of all;

> To see if any understand Your requirements,
>
> To see if any seek to know You.

The deniers turn from You,

> They do filthy things,
>
> They don't want to do good.

Do these deniers not understand what they do?

> They eat up good people like bread,
>
> They never call upon You.

Those who do right are afraid to deny You,

> They don't listen to the enemies;
>
> They put their trust in You, O Lord.

Come from Your home to save Your people.

> When you catch us away to take us home,

Jacob will rejoice in Your victory;

> Israel will be glad.

Amen

* A Psalm of David.

PSALM 15

*A Prayer That Asks God Who Are His Children**

Lord, who will live with You in Your Tabernacle in the holy hill?
  Those who follow Your principles,
  Those who do the right thing,
  Those who tell the truth,
  Those who do not lie about others,
  Those who do not sin against their friends,
  Those who recognize the enemies of God,
  Those who don't retaliate,
  Those who don't charge usury for loans,
  Those who don't take bribes?
Lord, honor those who fear Your name;
  Because they will live blamelessly for You.

Amen

*A Psalm of David.

PSALM 16

*A Prayer For Resurrection When Death Is Near**

Lord, keep me safe;
  Because I trust in You.
My soul said You are my Lord,
  Apart from You I have nothing to hope for.
Those who worship earthly gods will never find peace,
  I will not worship idols, nor confess them with my lips.
Lord, You are my future inheritance;
  You are my satisfaction Who will protect me in death.

You have given me a good life,

I follow the good heritage of my godly parents;

I bless You, Lord, for guiding me throughout life,

You showed me what to do in dark times.

I have always made You my guide,

I will not be shaken when death comes;

Because You have been at my right hand.

Now that I face death, I am satisfied;

I will die with great hope in Your resurrection,

You will not leave my soul in death,

Neither will You leave the Messiah in the grave.

You will raise us up to live again,

We will have fullness of joy in Your presence;

We will have pleasures forever.

Amen

*A Psalm by David carried on stone.

PSALM 17

*A Prayer For Victory As The Enemies Are Attacking**

Listen to the prayer of those who live right,

Answer my request to You, O Lord;

Because I am sincere when I pray.

Examine those who live right,

And You will know that I am blameless.

You have listened to the thoughts I think,

You visited me in the night to see if I sin.

You have examined me and found no rebellion,

That's because I determined that my mouth would not transgress.

I know the evil intent of those who hate You,
  So I stayed away from them.
Keep me in the right paths
  So that my feet won't slip.
I have called unto You because You are listening,
  Answer my request that I make.
Show Your wonderful love to me,
  And save me by Your strong hand
  From my enemies that attack me.

Keep me as the apple of Your eye,
  Hide me under the shadow of Your wing.
Because wicked people are ready to attack me,
  They have already surrounded me.
They are big and they are powerful,
  They brag that they will eliminate me.
Like a lion ready to pounce on its prey,
  They are ready to eat me up.

Come to my rescue, Lord, defend me;
  You can defeat the wicked.
They live for this world,
  They never think of others,
  They live to eat,
  They think only of themselves.
Lord, I will be happy when I see Your face;
  Then, I will be conformed into Your image.

                                    Amen

*A prayer of David.

PSALM 18

*A Prayer Of Thanksgiving For Deliverance From Danger**

Lord, I love You because You strengthen me;
   My rock, my fortress, my God.
Lord, I trust You because You save me;
   My high tower.
I will call upon You, because You are worthy to be praised;
   And You protect me from my enemies.
The threat of death scares me,
   The attack of the ungodly terrorizes me.
Lord, when I am afraid, I will call upon You;
   Even though You are in Your temple,
   You will hear me and give attention to my prayers.

Then You shook the earth so that it trembled,
   The hills moved because You were angry.
A flame of judgment came from Your mouth,
   You set on fire the surrounding hills,
You came down to us walking on the heavens,
   All darkness was crushed by Your feet.
You came flying to us upon the wind,
   Riding upon the clouds, You surrounded us.
You folded Your glory behind the darkness,
   You were accompanied by dark waters and thick clouds.
You are brightness and glory and fire,
   Yet You came to us in hailstones, lightning, and thunder.
Like an arrow of death, Your lightning struck them.
   You scared them, You killed them, You defeated them.
Then You sent the floods to wash them away,
   To judge them with Your anger.

You came from above to rescue me,
  To save me from drowning.
You saved me from a powerful enemy
  That was too strong for me,
  That hated everything I believed.
My enemy almost overwhelmed me,
  But You, Lord, saved me.
You lifted me into a secure place,
  You put Your delight in me.
Lord, You came to reward me;
  Because I have lived by Your principles,
  Because I have separated myself from sin.
You showed mercy to us who received Your mercy,
  You judged us righteously, who relied on Your righteousness.

You showed yourself pure, to those who sought Your purity;
  You showed yourself angry to those who were angry with You.
You saved those who are sorry for their sin,
  You punished those who refused to humble themselves.

Lord, light my candle so I can see;
  Take darkness away from my life.
By You, Lord, I can defeat a troop of men;
  With Your help I can jump over a wall.
Lord, Your principles for living are correct;
  Many have experimented with them,
  But You help all those who obey You.
Who is God, but You, Lord;
  Who is our stability, but You, Lord.
You make my feet sure like the mountain deer,
  You allow me to climb the heights.
You teach my hands how to fight,

So I can break the weapons of my enemies.
You have protected me with the shield of Your salvation,
 You have helped me to stand against my enemy;
 Your gentleness has made me strong.
You made my footsteps steady
 So that I did not slip and fall.
I chased my enemy and caught him,
 I did not quit until I defeated him.
I wounded him so that he could not fight back,
 I stomped on him with my feet.
You gave me strength to fight the battle,
 You defeated my enemies that hate You;
 You enabled me to destroy them.
The enemy cried out in pain,
 Their voices reached You in Heaven;
 But in hell it is too late for them.

I crushed the enemy so that they became dust,
 They were like the dirt in the street.
You have made me the leader of the heathen,
 I am above the people;
 Those I don't know will serve me.
They will obey my orders when they hear me,
 They will submit to my authority.
Strangers will be afraid of me,
 They will hide from me in their houses.

Lord, I bless You for giving me life and strength;
 I exalt you for giving me salvation,
Lord, You have delivered me over my enemies;
 You have given me authority over the people.
Therefore, among the heathen, I give You thanks;

I sing praises to Your name.

Lord, You have delivered Your king;

    You have shown mercy to David,

    You will preserve His seed forever.

Amen

*A Psalm of David the servant of the Lord, who spake unto the Lord the words of this song in the day that the Lord delivered him from the hand of all his enemies, and from the hand of Saul.

PSALM 19

*A Prayer For Wisdom So You Can Answer Doubters**

Lord, the heavens declare Your glory;

    The stars reveal Your craftsmanship.

Each new day tells You are the Creator,

    Each new night shows Your mighty power.

No one on earth can debate that You began all things,

    Because the universe answers all their arguments.

Your hand in creating the universe is seen everywhere,

    Your majestic plan extends to the last detail.

You made the night as a tent for the sun,

    Sunrise is like a bridegroom coming out of that tent.

The new day is like a runner beginning a marathon,

    The sun races from one horizon to the other.

The sun gives life to everything it touches.

Your Scripture, like the universe, is perfect;

    Converting the soul when applied.

Your principles never change,

    Making the ignorant wise when learned.

Fearing You takes away doubts and ignorance,

    Those who apply your truth live forever.

Your decisions are always accurate,

   Those who obey You live right.

Lord, Your truth is better than riches;

   Obeying Your principles is more satisfying than sweets.

Your truth keeps me on guard against danger,

   The satisfaction of obedience is its own reward.

Because no one is able to perceive their slightest deviation from truth,

   Therefore, keep me from making ignorant mistakes.

Also, keep me from making presumptuous errors;

   I don't want to be controlled by my faults.

I want to live blamelessly by Your principles,

   I want to be kept from making life-destroying decisions.

May the words that I speak,

   And the thoughts that I think,

Be acceptable to You, my Lord and my Redeemer.

Amen

*A Psalm of David.

PSALM 20

*A Prayer For Protection Against Opposition And A Prayer For Vindication When Doing The Right Things**

Lord, hear my prayers when pressures come;

   Defend me by the power of Your name.

Come to me with help from Your sanctuary,

   Give me strength to endure rejection.

Remember that I poured out my heart to You,

   And see that I come with a yielded spirit.

Give me what Your heart desires for me to have,
  Carry out Your plans in my life.

Then, I will rejoice when You save me;
  I will tell everyone what You have done,
  That You have carried out Your will in my life.

Now I know You care for Your chosen ones,
  You hear their prayers in Heaven;
  You save them by Your strong hand.

Some trust in chariots, some trust in horses;
  But I trust in Your name, Lord God.
Then will my enemies be defeated and eliminated,
  Then will I be vindicated and stand before You.

Save me, Lord, hear me when I call to You.

                                        Amen

*A Psalm of David.

PSALM 21

*A Prayer For Leaders To Defeat The Wicked**

Lord, I am encouraged when my leaders rejoice in You;
  When they shout "Amen" after a victory.
Lord, give my leaders what they want;
  Hold back nothing from them. Selah!
You rejoice with them when they have spiritual victories,
  You give them recognition and honor.
My leaders asked You to preserve their life,
  You answered their request;

You gave them long life.

Actually, it was Your victory they achieved,

    You gave them ability and success.

You gave them the enablement to win each victory,

    You give them the privilege of ruling for You.

But the leaders must trust in You,

    If they expect to keep their position.

You will defeat all Your enemies,

    Your strength will overcome all who hate You.

You will destroy them in a flaming furnace,

    You will consume them in hell's fire.

One day there will be no wicked people on earth,

    They and their descendants will be eliminated.

Although the wicked plot against Your principles,

    Their rebellious plans will not succeed.

The wicked will be completely defeated

    When You judge them.

I worship You for Your great strength,

    With singing I celebrate Your power.

                           Amen

*A Psalm of David.

PSALM 22

*A Prayer For Help When Being Attacked By Enemies**

My God, My God, why have You forsaken Me?

    Why are You so far away when I need You?

    Why don't You hear My agonizing prayer?

O God, You don't hear My prayers in the day;

    And in the night You are not near.

O God, You are the Holy One of Israel;
   You come to Your people when they worship You.

Our fathers trusted in You during troubled times,
   And You led them through their problems.
When they cried for deliverance,
   You gave them great victories.
But I am not equal to our fathers,
   People laugh at Me and hate Me.
They reject Me openly to My face,
   They make fun of Me in front of others.
They think I'm crazy for putting My trust in You,
   They tell Me You won't come to Me in trouble;
   Nor will You vindicate Me.

But You are the One who formed Me in the womb,
   You set Me apart for a special task when I was a baby.
I've had My trust in You since I was born,
   O God, You are the only hope I've got.
So don't cut Me off from Your protection,
   I don't have another way to solve My problems.
My enemies are smart and they are powerful,
   They attack Me at My weaknesses.
Their accusations and lies are tearing Me up,
   Their words hurt more than physical suffering.

My spirit is crushed and I don't want to live,
   Evil pressure is worse than physical suffering.
When My soul is attacked by the enemy's warfare,
   My body aches all over and I want to give up.
I don't know what to say.
   Why have You allowed these trials to attack Me?

Like wild dogs, the enemy is chewing Me up,
 They are trying to kill Me.
They are nailing Me to a cross,
 All My bones ache from being pulled out of joint.
They have stolen everything from Me,
 And they are gambling over My clothes.

O Lord, don't stand so far away from Me;
 Come near Me to help Me through this difficulty.
Give Me inner strength to stand up to them
 And give me inner confidence to overcome their tricks.

I will tell everyone how You came to Me,
 I will testify of Your goodness to other believers.
They need to know that You take care of those that trust You,
 They need to trust You as I do.
Because You will come to us when we are in trouble,
 You will not hide Your face from us when we need You.
I will praise You to other believers,
 I will do everything that I promised.
Then weak Christians will be encouraged to trust You,
 They will continue following You throughout their life.
The unsaved will recognize what You do for Your children,
 And they will turn to You for salvation.

Your kingdom shall come on earth one day,
 And Your rule will be recognized by all.
Your children will enjoy Your kingdom and worship You,
 But the unsaved cannot escape Your coming judgment.

There will always be a small remnant who serves You,
 They are the ones You recognize and protect.

They will declare to all how You take care of Your children,
And each new generation will contain more believers
Who will also declare Your goodness and care.

Amen

*A Psalm of David.

PSALM 23

*A Prayer Recognizing God's Protective Relationship To You**

Lord, You are my Shepherd,
I don't need anything.
You make me lie down in green pastures,
You lead me beside still waters.
You renew my spiritual energy,
You guide me in the right paths;
To glorify Your name.

When I walk through dark valleys,
I will not be afraid of death shadows.
Because You are with me,
Your rod and staff protect me.

You prepare a banquet table for me,
And my enemies watch me eat.
You pour oil on my head to honor and heal me,
You fill my cup so it runs over.
Surely your goodness and mercy will follow me,
As long as I live on this earth;
And in eternity I will live in Your house forever.

Amen

*A Psalm of David.

PSALM 24

*A Prayer For Your Final Recognition And Triumph Over The Enemy**

Lord, You cause Your earth to give good things,
    You also own everyone who lives on this earth.
You created the earth as a watery sphere,
    And on the first day, You divided the waters from the land.

Who can come into Your presence, O Lord;
    Who is able to stand before You?
Only those who have clean hands and a pure heart,
    Those who separate themselves from sin.

Those standing in Your presence receive Your blessings,
    You declare them righteous through salvation.
These are the ones who seek to know You,
    These are the ones who want to stand in Your presence. Selah!

Lord, I know You will open wide the eternal gates;
    Enter because You are the King of glory.
Your enemies ask, "Who is the King of glory?"
    You are the Lord, mighty to destroy them.

So march through the eternal gates,
    Enter triumphantly, my King of glory.
In judgment they continue to ask, "Who is the King of glory?"
    The Creator of all the universe is the King of glory. Selah!

Amen

*A Psalm of David.

PSALM 25

*A Prayer Of The Weak Believer For Help In Trouble**

Unto You, O Lord, do I come in prayer;
   O God, I trust You; do not let me be embarrassed;
   Nor let me be defeated by my enemies.

Lord, don't let any of Your children be embarrassed
   Because they put their trust in You;
   Let those who rebel against You be embarrassed.

Show me the principles to follow in life,
   Teach me to obey Your truth.
Make me follow Your principles,
   Because You are the God that has salvation;
   I come to You for my deliverance.

Lord, remember Your tender mercies for me;
   You have always shown Your love to me.
Don't remember the sins I commit as a youth,
   O Lord, deal with me according to Your mercy.

Lord, in Your goodness, You always do right;
   Therefore, make rebels obey Your way of living.
I know You will take care of the meek in judgment,
   And You will teach them how to obey Your way.
You always do the right thing,
   You show mercy to those who obey Your principles.

Forgive me my sin for Your name's sake,

Because I have not been perfect in many ways.
The ones who will fear Your name,
   Guide them to do the right things.
Give them peace because of their obedience,
   Let their children prosper.

Lord, I know You have the secret to life;
   You have agreed to give life to those who obey You.
Lord, I always look to You for deliverance;
   You will lead me through trouble.

Make me always look to You for future deliverance,
   Sometimes I am too dumb and weak to do it.
My heart deceives me about decisions,
   Make me follow You out of my problems.

I have many enemies that hate me,
   They want to destroy me.
Keep me close to You when trials come,
   I don't want to be embarrassed;
   I trust You to deliver me.

Help me always tell the truth,
   And guide me to always do the right thing.
Save Your people out of their trouble.

                              Amen

*A Psalm of David.

PSALM 26

*A Prayer Of A Conscientious Believer That He/She Is Sincere**

O Lord, examine me to see my integrity;
  Because when I put my trust in You, I did not slip.
Examine my intentions thoroughly,
  Because I have not willingly sinned in my thoughts and intents.
I have meditated on Your love to me,
  And I have tried to live by Your principles.

I have not listened to Your enemies,
  Neither have I had fellowship with them.
I don't hang out with those who disobey You,
  And I do not let them influence me.
I have tried to always live innocently,
  Therefore I walk in Your forgiveness.
I tell everyone I am thankful for You,
  And that I am grateful for Your work in my life.

Lord, I have to come into Your presence,
  To spend time with You in Your home.
Don't lump me in with disobedient sinners,
  Nor with murderers who take innocent lives.
They constantly reject Your truth,
  They lie when they break Your law.
As for me, I will be true to my integrity,
  Redeem me because of Your mercy.
I know I am on solid ground,
  So I join other believers to bless You, Lord.

                                        Amen

*A Psalm of David.

PSALM 27

*A Prayer To Be In God's Presence For Protection**

Lord, You are my light and my salvation;
  Whom shall I fear?
Lord, You are the strength of my life;
  Why should I be afraid?
When evil persons come to eat me up,
  They stumble and fall.
Though a host of evil people attack me,
  I will not be afraid of them;
  Because I know You will protect me.

Lord, there's one thing I want from You;
  I want to be in Your house to see Your beauty,
  I want to delight in Your presence.
Lord, when troubles and problems attack me;
  Hide me in Your presence,
  Set me on a rock so my enemies can't reach me.
Lord, lift me up above my enemies;
  I will bring the sacrifices of joy to You,
  I will sing praises to You.

O Lord, hear when I cry unto You;
  Send me the help I need.
When You said to me, "Seek My face,"
  I answered, "Your face will I seek."
Don't hide Your face when I'm searching for You,
  I need You, because only You can save me.
Even if my mother and father forsake me,
  I know You will not leave me.

Lord, teach me how to successfully follow Your way;

  Because my enemies are waiting to attack me.

Lord, don't let my enemies capture me,

   Because they tell lies about me, and threaten my life.

I would have fainted and given up

   If it hadn't been for Your goodness to me.

Lord, I will wait courageously for You because

   I know You will deliver me;

   I know You will come to me.

Amen

*A Psalm of David.

PSALM 28

A Request For God To Hear
*Your Prayer When The Wicked Oppose You**

Lord, I pray to You for help, don't be silent;

   If You don't hear and answer my prayer,

   I'll be like the unsaved who can't pray.

Hear my prayers when I plead with You,

   When I stretch out my hands toward Your presence.

Don't treat me like You treat the wicked,

   Who lie and violate Your principles.

Judge them because they commit sin,

   Punish them with the anguish they curse others.

The wicked do not live by Your principles,

   Nor do they care how You run the world;

   They destroy all that You've done.

Lord, I bless You for hearing my prayers,

    You are my strength and protector.

Because I trusted You, I was delivered,

    Therefore I sing praises for Your protection.

Lord, You give me ability to overcome difficulties;

    Just as You gave Your Anointed strength during His suffering.

Save Your people and bless them with Your presence,

    Give them food to eat on life's journey;

    And when they die take them to Your eternal home.

Amen

*A Psalm of David.

PSALM 29

*A Prayer That Is Revealed In A Thunder Storm Glorifying God For His Power**

Lord, I glorify You because of Your awesome creation;

    I recognize Your demonstrated power in this created world.

Lord, all of us who enjoy this earth

    Are obligated to worship You because it reflects the beauty
of Your holiness.

Lord, I hear You speak in the sound of powerful rivers;

    I hear Your thunder in the storms,

    Your presence is felt when the floods sweep things away.

I am awed by Your powerful voice in the storm,

    Your presence is majestic and compelling.

Lord, You speak when storms uproot trees;

    You speak when trees are snapped and broken.

Your storms skip playfully through meadows like a calf,

    Your winds tear up the bushes like a young ox.

Your voice pierces like the lightning,

Your voice like the wind sweeps across the desert.

You speak when the oaks are broken,

And Your sound is heard as the forest is stripped bare.

All in Your temple cry "glory!"

Because You rule over the storms.

You sit enthroned in Heaven,

You rule over all that happens on earth.

Lord, You give me strength

To live through the storms of life;

You give me inner peace while the storms rage.

Amen

*A Psalm of David.

PSALM 30

*A Prayer Of Gratitude To God For Good Health**

Lord, I lift You up because You have protected me;

You have not allowed the enemy of death to conquer me.

When I was sick, I begged You to let me live;

And You healed me.

Lord, You delivered me from dying;

You kept me alive for a purpose.

I sing unto You, O Lord, with the saints,

And remember Your majestic holiness.

You have allowed me to be sick for only a moment,

And now You have allowed me to live.

I wept throughout the night,

But joy came in the morning.

When I was healthy, I thought I'd live forever;

I said I shall never get sick.

Now I realize I live by Your pleasure,

    You have made me as strong as a mountain.

When You withheld Your spiritual blessings from me,

    I was scared that I might die.

Then I begged You to let me live,

    I prayed for You to hear me.

I said there is no reason for me to die,

    Because I cannot praise You if I am in the grave.

Hear my urgent prayer for mercy,

    Come heal me in my hour of need.

Thank You for turning my mourning into dancing,

    You let me take off my hospital gown and put on happiness.

I want my healing to praise You,

    O Lord, my God, I give You thanks forever.

                               Amen

*A Psalm and song at the dedication of the house of David.

HOW TO PRAY

When Facing An Enemy:
Psalm 31

When I face an enemy, I feel scared, and I don't like feeling terrified. I pray about my anxiety, "Don't let me be embarrassed; come down here to listen to me; I need You quickly" (v. 1-2, PTP). *Here I am, Lord; I need You now.*

It's hard to get my attention off my oppressors. They seem so strong, and the fact I'm distressed shows they have the upper hand right now. "I hate those who tell lies" (v. 6, PTP). "My enemies keep chewing on me" (v. 11, PTP). When I focus on my adversary, I don't have my focus on the Lord. "I want to see Your face; in Your mercy protect me" (v. 16, PTP). *Lord, when I look at trouble, it's hard to think about You. Help me look beyond my trouble to see You.*

I need to trust in God's plan for my life, even in my difficulties. I need to know that the Lord will keep me when I'm going through danger, even though I'm hurt. "Lord, I bless You for Your mercy, because You protect me from all kinds of danger" (v. 21, PTP). *Lord, I yield to Your plan; lead me today.*

When I face an enemy, I need to be courageous. But strength is not within. "Lord, make me courageous in the face of lies, strengthen me to deal with them" (v. 24, PTP). Sometimes I get mad at them, but that's not courage. When I get angry, I just give in to my emotions. When I react "shut up their lying mouth," (v. 18, PTP), *Lord, look beyond my angry petition and show me Your presence.* "Give me access to Your secret presence" (v. 20, PTP). *Here I come, Lord.*

When I face an enemy, I need to trust the Lord. "You are the only One I can trust, You are my Lord and my God" (v. 14, PTP). When I don't have courage or self-control and I am so frustrated I don't know what to do, I need to trust the Lord. "Strengthen me to deal with them, because I put my hope in You" (v. 24, PTP).

PSALM 31

*A Prayer To Help You Face The Lies Of Your Enemy**

Lord, I trust You to deliver me;
   Don't let me be embarrassed.
Come down here to listen to me,
   I need You quickly.

I need You to be as strong as a rock,
   To keep me from being defeated.
I need to hold Your hand,
   So You can lead me out of this trouble.

Get me out of this predicament,
   I know You can do it.
I put myself into Your hands,
   Because You are my Redeemer.

I hate those who tell lies,
   Because I serve You, the God of truth.

I happily depend upon Your mercy
   Because You know the mess I'm in,
   And You know how miserable I feel.
You have not boxed me in with my enemies,
   You have given me lots of space.

Please be merciful to me in my trouble,
   Because I am eaten up with anxiety.
My eyes are swollen from crying,
   I'm so tired I can't do anything.

My enemies kept chewing on me,
    Even my friends turned against me;
    They avoided me, walking the other way.

No one cares what happens to me,
    I am thrown in the trash like a broken glass.
When I heard the lies my enemies told about me,
    It scared me to death.
Then my enemies began planning together
    How to get rid of me.

You are the only One I can trust,
    You are my Lord and my God.
I commit my life to You.
    Deliver me from my enemies who hate me,
    And from those who are trying to get me.

I want to see Your face,
    In Your mercy protect me.
Lord, I don't want to be embarrassed;
    I ask You to protect me.

Embarrass my enemies, O Lord,
    And confuse their plans against me.
Shut up their lying mouth,
    So they can't tell lies against those who live by Your principles.

Lord, You are so good to me when I obey You;
    Therefore I trust You with my reputation.
Give me access to Your secret presence,
    I feel protected when I'm near You.
Lord, I bless You for Your mercy;

Because You protect me from all kinds of danger.

I'm sorry for complaining about being cut off,

But in spite of my complaint, You answered me.

Lord, I love You for protecting me;

And for punishing those who lie about me.

Lord, make me courageous in the face of lies;

Strengthen me to deal with them,

Because I put my hope in You.

Amen

*A Psalm of David.

PSALM 32

A Prayer For Forgiveness After Committing Sin

Lord, I am blessed;

Because You forgave all my rebellion,

Lord, I am blessed;

Because You cover my sin,

Now I can enjoy Your presence.

You bless me by erasing my errors from Your books,

You don't even remember them.

When I refused to recognize my sin,

My whole body cried out with conviction.

Day and night my guilt racked me with pain,

My mouth was so dry I couldn't speak. Selah!

I recognize my sin that made me a wreck,

I can no longer hide my faults from You. Selah!

So I confessed my transgression to You and repented,
   Then You forgave my terrible sin.

Because You are gracious to forgive our iniquity,
   Every godly person will rest securely in You,
   When judgment comes upon us.
I will hide in You when that day comes,
   I will worship You with songs of deliverance. Selah!

Lord, teach me the proper principles of living;
   Guide me so I don't make mistakes.
I don't want to be like a horse that can't understand,
   So You have to jerk me about with a bit in my mouth.

Those who rebel against You have a hard life,
   But You show mercy to those who trust You.
I am happy because I follow Your principles,
   And I shout for joy because You make me do right.

                                        Amen

*A Psalm of instruction by David.

PSALM 33

A Prayer For God To Bless Sincere People

Lord, I rejoice because You allowed me to approach You;
   I worship You as I come to You.
Everyone should praise You, Lord, with stringed instruments;
   With instruments we should magnify You.
I write new songs to worship You,
   I sing praises to You from the bottom of my heart;

Because everything You say is right,
Everything You do is perfect.

You love to do right things and make right decisions,
You have made everything on earth good.
You spoke and the hemisphere just appeared,
You breathed life into all the angels.
You scooped all the earth's water into Your hands,
You planned the deepest part of the oceans.

Therefore, everyone on earth ought to recognize Your power;
They should be afraid of Your authority.
Everything You spoke was done just like You said,
Everything happened just as You wanted it to happen.

Lord, You mess up the plans of the ungodly;
When they try to go against Your principles.
Lord, Your decisions are always right;
Anyone who wants to can know Your principles.
You will always bless any group that follows Your laws,
You will make them Your people.

You look down to find conscientious worshippers,
You examine every heart to see who is sincere;
Not a single person escapes Your scrutiny.

You gave everyone the same opportunity to seek You,
Now You want to see what they have done with their chances.
No leader is saved just because he has a big following,
You do not save anyone by their ability.
No one can put their trust in earthly transportation,
Because that won't get anyone into Your presence.

You see everyone who reverently follows You.

    You know those who trust in Your mercy.

You will deliver their soul from hell,

    You will take care of them on this earth.

I humbly wait for Your blessing,

    You are my help and my protection.

I will rejoice in what You give me,

    Because I trust You to protect me and give me good things.

Lord, show me Your mercy in this life;

    Because You are the only one I can trust.

Amen

PSALM 34

*A Prayer Of Gratitude For Deliverance From Trouble**

I will worship You, Lord, at all times;

    Your praise will continually be in my mouth.

I will tell everyone that I trust in You,

    Those who hardly obey You will rejoice with me.

Lord, I magnify Your greatness;

    I want everyone to join me in praising You.

I searched for You when I was scared to death,

    You took away my anxiety.

Others looked to You when they were afraid,

    You did not disappoint them.

When I was scared, I cried to You for help;

    You heard me and delivered me from all my troubles.

You sent angels to protect me,
  You told them to surround me and deliver me.

I have eaten the good food You provide,
  Thank You for satisfying me with Your presence.
I want all Your children to trust You,
  Because I know You will take care of them.

The young rebellious lions go hungry,
  But Your children enjoy the good things You give.
So I want everyone to listen to me,
  Because I can teach them how to find satisfaction.

Lord, I know the average person doesn't want to die;
  They want to live a long time and have a good life.
To get it they must quit speaking evil,
  And begin seeking the truth found in You.
They must repent of their evil ways,
  And live peacefully according to Your principles.

I know You see everything that Your children do,
  And You hear everything that they say.
But Your face is against those who do evil,
  They die and You kick them out of Your presence.

Your children that live right cry to You,
  And You deliver them out of all their troubles.
You are near to those who have a broken heart,
  You save those who are sorry for their sin.

I know we who try to live right have many afflictions,
  But You deliver us out of them all.

You protect us when they want to kill us,

    They don't do us any permanent harm.

The sinners will agonize in their sins,

    Those that hate peace-loving people will never have peace.

But You will redeem the life of us who serve You;

    You will never abandon us.

Amen

*A Psalm of David, when he changed his behavior before Abimelech, who drove him away, and he departed.

PSALM 35

A Prayer For God To Intervene When "Friends" Lie About You

Lord, I want You on my side;

    Against those who are out to get me.

Protect my back side against my enemies,

    And oppose their evil plans against me.

Use their lying tactics to confuse them,

    And give me confidence to deal with them.

Undermine their arrogance and evil determination,

    Make them suffer the humiliation they plan against me.

Cut them down like weeds,

    And let Your angels blow them away like the wind.

Blind them so they stagger like a blind person,

    Let Your angels punish them.

My enemies didn't have any reason to attack me.

    I didn't do anything to make them mad.

So punish them when they don't know it's coming,
>   Just like they attacked me when I didn't expect it.

I rejoice in You, Lord,
>   Because You have saved me from my enemies.
I thank You deeply for delivering me,
>   From an enemy that was too strong for me.
They lied about me behind my back,
>   I didn't even know they were plotting against me.
I had been kind to them and helped them,
>   But they returned evil for the good I did for them.
When they were in trouble,
>   I spent my time praying for them;
I went without food fasting for them,
>   Did I waste my time caring about them?

I treated them like a friend,
>   I pledged myself to them with a handshake.
But when I got in trouble,
>   They spread bad news about me when I wasn't around.
I didn't know they were plotting against me,
>   They did everything possible to destroy me.
To my face they were hypocrites,
>   But behind my back they ripped me to shreds.

Lord, are You going to just watch their treachery from Heaven?
>   Come help me in my struggle against them.
Then I will tell all who trust You,
>   How You defeated them to save me.
Don't let my enemies be the ones rejoicing,
>   Make them howl with pain for what they've done.
Because they don't want to follow You,

They want to turn Your followers against each other.
They keep pointing out my troubles to other people,
　　Saying I deserve to be punished.

Lord, You've seen what they've done to me;
　　Don't keep still in Heaven,
　　Don't turn Your back on me.
Get up and do something about it,
　　Come to my defense, O Lord.
Examine me to see if I am sincerely following You,
　　Don't listen to their lies about me.
Don't let them convince others I am a fraud,
　　Don't let them eat me up.
Embarrass them because they lied about me,
　　They tried to make me look bad;
　　Now let everyone see their lies and hypocrisy.

Lord, let Your followers rejoice because You step in;
　　Let them know that You will do the right thing,
　　And that You will punish those who will not follow You.
Lord, I praise You because You will do right;
　　I will praise You all day long.

                                        Amen

*A Psalm of David.

PSALM 36

A Prayer That Explains The Difference
*Between Godly And Rebellious People**

Lord, I know the wicked reject You in their hearts;
　　The way they live shows they do not fear You.

They live to glorify themselves,

And their pride is despicable.

They only curse or deceive others,

They can't do good things because they are rebellious.

They constantly think up evil things to do,

And they are not sorry when they break Your laws.

Lord, Your mercy lets all people live;

You are continually faithful to this plan.

You are the source of how to live right,

And You allow all people to live out their life.

Your love to all is perfect,

Therefore, Your children trust You to protect them.

You give them the purpose to live,

You let them drink until they are satisfied from Your rivers.

Lord, You are the source of life;

You give us light to guide our life.

Continue loving those that obey Your principles,

And help them live right according to Your standards.

Don't let arrogant people attack me,

And keep them from destroying me.

They will fail because of their sin,

And when they die, they will not live in Your presence.

Amen

*A Psalm of David the servant of the Lord.

PSALM 37

A Prayer Thanking God For His Protection Of Good People And His Punishment Of Wicked People*

Lord, I'm not going to worry about lawbreakers;
   Because I don't care what they get illegally.
They will soon dry up like cut grass,
   They will eventually die just like new flowers wither.
Lord, I put my trust in You and I live right;
   I know You'll protect me and provide for me.
You satisfy me more than anything else,
   And You fulfill every desire of my heart.

I commit my days' activities to You,
   I know You will work everything out.
You will make my sincerity bright like a sunrise,
   My decisions will shine like the noonday.
Lord, I rest in Your presence;
   I wait patiently for Your guidance.

I won't worry about those who make money
   Off their illegal deals,
Lord, I've stopped getting mad at those who cheat,
   And I don't envy those who get ahead unlawfully,
   Because You will eventually cut them off.
But You will prosper those who follow You,
   It won't be long till You get rid of deceivers;
   And those who care about them won't be able to find them.

But the meek will be rewarded by You,
   Then will they live happy and secure lives.

The lawbreakers plan to deceive Your children,
    And they tell lies about them.
But You just laugh at them,
    Because You know payday is coming soon.
The wicked have made elaborate plans to defraud Your followers,
    And to steal everything that they possess.
Lord, use their cheating ways against them;
    May they lose everything they have stolen.

I know it is better to be godly with a little,
    Than to get rich off evil schemes.
You cut off the wretched hand that tries to steal,
    While You are protecting Your children.
You take care of Your children each day,
    And You give them a reward they will never lose.
They will not be ashamed when You judge them,
    And in difficult times You will provide for them.

But Your enemies shall be burnt up,
    They shall just disappear like smoke.
They take from us and never give anything back,
    But Your children are kind and genuine.
They shall eventually inherit the earth,
    You will not judge them or cut them off.

You direct the steps of good people,
    As they delight to follow Your principles.
Good people do not stay down when they are knocked down,
    You help them get up each time.
Lord, You have let me live from infancy till I am old;
    I have never seen You turn Your back on Your children,
    You have always taken care of Your own.

Lord, help Your followers to not follow evil;

But help them always follow good principles.

Because You will love those who do right,

You never forsake them who follow You;

You will cut off those who do wickedness.

Those who do right will inherit the earth one day,

They will live there forever with You.

They will always say the right things,

They will tell everyone that You do right things.

They will live by Your laws,

Their feet will not be tripped up by sin.

The wicked will keep their eye on Your children,

Looking for ways to trip them up.

But You will not abandon Your followers to evil people,

You will remember them when judgment comes.

Lord, I wait on You and try to obey You;

I know I will inherit the earth with Your children,

But You will cut off the wicked.

Lord, the wicked seem to have great influence;

They seem to prosper like a spreading oak tree.

But I know they will pass away,

One day I won't be able to find them anywhere.

Lord, watch the one who obeys Your principles;

Because that one will make peace.

But the disobedient will be altogether destroyed,

They will be completely cut off.

You will save those who do right,

You will strengthen them when trouble comes.

You will help them make it through difficult times,

You will deliver them from wicked ones;
Because they trust in You.

                              Amen

*A Psalm of David.

PSALM 38

The Prayer Of A Person Who Is Suffering Because He Did Wrong

O Lord, don't fuss at me when I've made You angry;
    And don't punish me because I've disobeyed You.
I can't forget about Your punishment,
    Your hand stings me because of my wrong.
I don't have the strength to endure Your punishment,
    I can't find rest because of my sin.
Because my rebellion brought this all on me,
    Now this is too heavy to bear.
My wounds where You punish me are infected,
    I am hurting because of my stubbornness;
    I am troubled,
    I cry all the time.
My miserable body aches all over,
    I am not getting any better.
My rebellious spirit is broken,
    And I have no will to go on living.
I don't have any more love in my heart,
    And I don't have any ambition.
My friends have all forsaken me,
    And my family doesn't even come around any more.

My enemies are still trying to destroy me,
   They lie about me behind my back.
Because I don't care about anything,
   I don't listen to what they say;
   I don't even try to defend myself.

Lord, You are the only thing I have left;
   I know You will listen to me.
Don't let my enemies gloat over my misfortune,
   Don't let them use my weaknesses to their advantage.
I'm ready to give up,
   Because I messed up so bad.
I recognize I've disobeyed You,
   I am sorry for my sin.
My enemies jump on every opportunity,
   Every day more join them to attack me.
They never consider anything I've done right,
   They render evil for the good I've done.

Lord, don't leave me now;
   Don't keep Your distance.
Come quick to help me;
   Lord, You are my salvation.

                            Amen

*A Psalm of remembrance by David.

HOW TO PRAY

When You Need Guidance:
Psalm 39

There comes a time when you need God's direction in your life. Maybe you've made a mistake, maybe you've sinned and are in trouble, maybe you just haven't been listening to God. But now you need God to show you what to do. So pray with the Psalmist, "Lead me and guide me" (Ps. 31:3). Hasn't God promised, "I will instruct you and teach you in the way you should go; I will guide you with My eye" (Ps. 32:8)? *Lord, I claim Your promise, show me what to do.*

The first step to find God's will for your life is to take responsibility for your life. No one else will answer to God for your action; even God Himself holds you responsible. "I will guard my ways, lest I sin" (Ps. 39:1). *Lord, no one else can properly tell me what to do. I listen to You.*

The second step in finding guidance is meditation. The Psalmist said, "My heart was hot within me; while I was musing, the fire burned" (Ps. 39:3). Because the Psalmist was agitated or worried, he began thinking about a solution to his problem. But thinking is not enough, you've got to think about God's solution to your dilemma. *Lord, I come to You because I don't know what to do.*

The third thing is to ask God for direction. "Lord, make me to know my end" (Ps. 39:4). Remember, the New Testament exhorts, "You do not have because you do not ask" (Jas. 4:2). *Lord, if I've never asked You to guide my life, I do it now. Show me what to do; I will do it.*

Next, realize God is in control, even though you think everything is out of control. The Psalmist told God, "You have made my days" (Ps. 39:5). Even though you are in trouble, you can't help yourself. "Every man at his best state is but vapor" (Ps. 39:5).

The fifth thing is to ask God to help you keep from making mistakes. And when you do make mistakes, ask God to help you overcome their consequences. "Deliver me from the consequences of my sin" (Ps. 39:8, PTP). *Lord, I will do what I think You want me to do. Protect me from bad judgment and accidents.*

The sixth thing is to ask for God's strength to do the things He directs. Many people pray for God's guidance, but after they know what to do, they won't do it (disobedience) or they can't do it (inability). "Lord, I'm just a traveler in this life ... spare me from the afflictions, so I can get strong again" (Ps. 39:13, PTP).

Trust in the Lord, and do good; dwell in the land, and feed on His faithfulness. Delight yourself also in the Lord, and He shall give you the desires of your heart. Commit your way to the Lord, trust also in Him, and He shall bring it to pass (Ps. 37:3-5).

PSALM 39

*A Prayer To Use Opportunities Wisely In This Short Life**

Lord, I will pay attention to how I live;
> I will not sin with my words.
I will be careful what I say,
> Especially when I'm around non-Christian people.
I was speechless because I was accomplishing so little,
> But inwardly I was about to explode.
My heart burned with fire as I thought about it,
> Then I had to admit my weaknesses.

Lord, help me understand what's happening to me;
> And help me use my time wisely,
> I know my weaknesses.
Lord, You have given me a certain amount of time;
> My life span is short compared to You,
> Even when I do my best, it's insignificant. Selah!

I'm like others who also do insignificant things;
    They are not satisfied with their accomplishments,
    They build up a nest egg but someone else spends it.
So Lord, I look for satisfaction in You;
    My hope is in You.

Deliver me from the consequence of my sin,
    Don't let non-Christians ridicule me.
Now I refused to complain any more,
    Because You answered my prayer.
Take away Your punishment from me,
    I am about to die from it.
You do not take away my life because of my sin,
    Yet my beautiful youth is fading away;
    Because that is the destiny of mankind. Selah!

O Lord, listen to my request;
    I am crying because You are far away,
    I'm just a traveler in this life like those before me.
Spare me from afflictions so I can get strong,
    Because I'll soon die and leave this earth.

Amen

*A Psalm of David.

PSALM 40

*A Prayer For Help In Times Of Difficulties**

Lord, I wait patiently for You;
    Listen to me and hear my request.
You brought me up out of a horrible pit,
    You set me on a rock and established my life.

You put a new song in my heart,
　　Even praise to You for delivering me.
Many will hear my song of worship to You,
　　They will also put their trust in You.

You bless all those who trust You for salvation,
　　And those who repent from their lies and arrogance.
Lord, You have done many wonderful works;
　　You have kept me in Your thoughts.

I cannot understand all You do for me,
　　The things You do for me cannot be remembered.
You do not want me to bring sacrifices to You,
　　I come to You the way You command in Scripture.

You want me to obey Your will,
　　My heart delights to do Your command.
I have told everyone to live right,
　　You know I was never ashamed to testify for You.

I have not been a "secret believer,"
　　You know I told everyone about Your faithfulness to me.
I didn't keep quiet about my faith,
　　I told everyone I was Your follower.

Therefore, don't withhold Your tender mercy from me;
　　Lord, preserve me as You have promised.
There are so many temptations I can't count them,
　　They make me feel guilty and discouraged.

Lord, please come deliver me from the evil one;
    Come quickly, I need You now.
Embarrass them that are trying to defeat me,
    Let them suffer the defeat they plan for me.

Let them experience the misery of their sin
    That they plan for me to experience.
Let all that seek You rejoice in Your salvation,
    Let them have the pleasure of magnifying You continually.

Lord, You know I am poor and needy;
    Look to me in my time of need.
Come help me get through my difficulties,
    Come quickly, God, because I need You now.

                                                      Amen

*A Psalm of David.

PSALM 41

*A Prayer For Healing So Your Enemies Won't Spread Gossip That You Are Sick**

Lord, You bless those who look after the poor;
    You promise to deliver those who defend the poor.
You promised to preserve that person's life,
    And You will not deliver them to their enemies.
When that person gets sick, You will take care of them;
    You will be with them in their illness.

Now I am that person who needs Your mercy,
    Heal me, even though I have sinned against You.

My enemies tell everyone about my troubles,
    They are anxious for me to die.
They lie when they come to pay a sick call on me,
    They are just gathering gossip to spread to my enemies.

Everyone that hates me continues to spread dirt,
    So they can destroy my reputation and my life.
They claim I am about to die because of my sin,
    And that I cannot recover from this problem.
Even some close friends that I used to trust,
    Are trying to knife me in the back.

Now Lord, be merciful to me in my sickness;
    Raise me up so I can go after them.
When You raise me up it will be a signal
    That my enemies cannot defeat me.
I know You will judge me with integrity,
    And that I will enjoy Your presence.
I bless You, the Lord of Israel,
    You are the same from everlasting to everlasting.
                                    Amen and Amen
*A Psalm of David.

HOW TO PRAY

When You Want To Know God:
The Sons of Korah Psalms

The passion of the sons of Korah was to know God intimately. These are the Psalms to pray when you feel separated from God, alienated, or alone. Perhaps the sons of Korah continually sought the presence of God, because their family namesake wouldn't come to the Tabernacle. He alienated himself from God.

Originally, Korah was born into the family of Levi and became a priest of God (see Ex. 6:24). He was a young man delivered from slavery in Egypt. Korah saw the power of God when he walked through the Red Sea on dry land. He ate the manna that was supernaturally supplied by God, and drank the water from the rock. He had seen one miracle after another. As a priest, Korah sacrificed to God for his sins, as well as for the sins of his family and others.

But Moses and Aaron became the leaders of God's people, not Korah. Korah became jealous, and along with two of his companions, Dathan and Abiram, they resisted Moses' leadership (see Num. 16; 26:9-11; 27:3; Jude 11). God saw the sin of Korah and commanded him to appear before the Lord at the Tabernacle. But Korah, Dathan, and Abiram refused to obey the Lord and were swallowed up by the earth in an earthquake. However, his sons were spared (see Num. 26:11). *Lord, help me learn to obey when I see others rebel against You.*

What does this mean? Apparently, the sons of Korah were ashamed of their father's rebellion to God. In reaction, they became meek and obedient to the Lord. Because their father refused to come to the Tabernacle, the sons of Korah stayed as close to the Tabernacle as possible. Never again did a son of Korah become a prideful leader. They served the Lord without recognition or fanfare. Therefore, when they wrote a Psalm, it was about knowing God. They didn't attach their individual names; rather, their Psalms are ascribed to "the sons of Korah." *Lord, I pray what they prayed; "I'd rather be a doorkeeper in Your house, than to live sumptuously in the tents of wickedness"* (Ps. 84:10, PTP).

Praying Their Psalms

The sons of Korah saw God everywhere, and they passionately desired to experience His presence. The story is told of two priests from the sons of Korah who had been away from the Temple for a long time. They had not been able to sacrifice to God, nor to hear the great psalms sung by the Levitical choir in the Temple. As they were returning through the wilderness, they saw a young deer being chased through the woods by dogs. It is here that the sons of Korah wrote:

As a young deer, running through the woods looking for water,

So pants my soul after Thee, O God,

My soul is thirsty for God.

I have been away from Thy Temple, now I want to worship my God,

I want to appear in the presence of God,

I want to pour out my soul to God.

They saw my discouragement and said, where is your God?

As deep calls to deep, I call to God,

I will go up with worshippers this day.

Psalm 42:1-3, 7 (AMP)

Psalm 48, written by the sons of Korah, focuses your attention on two great attributes of God: first, His great power, and second, His loving kindness. His power is emphasized in verses 1-8, and His love is seen in verses 9-14. The word *Selah* in verse 8 separates the two sections. When you praise God for His greatness, you end by saying "Selah," a word that suggests, "think" or "time out to meditate on God." *Lord, help me forget about things, when I think on You.*

The sons of Korah loved the Temple and the city of Jerusalem. They wrote, "Great is the Lord . . . in the city of our God, in His holy mountain" (Ps. 48:1). "The joy of the whole earth is Mount Zion . . . the city of the great king" (vs. 2). They loved Jerusalem and its palaces, and seeing where the king passed by, but most of all "the city of the Lord of hosts ... the city of our God" (vs. 8). *Lord, I yearn for Your city, the new Heaven and the new earth* (Rev. 21:1).

The courts of the Temple are where the sons of Korah experienced God. They loved to serve God in the Temple, because He was there.

> How amiable is Your Temple, O Lord God of hosts,
>> My soul longs for Your courts,
>> My heart cries out for the Living God.
> Yes, the sparrow must find a house for its young,
>> My home is with my God,
>> Even with Your altar, my God.
> Blessed are all who desire to dwell in Your house,
>> They go from strength to strength.
>> Every one to appear before God.
> I'd rather be in Your court one day, than any other
> place one thousand,
>> I'd rather be a doorkeeper in God's house,
>> Than be rich in the tents of wickedness.
> God protect me, be my sun and shield,
>> Lord give me grace and glory,
>> Don't keep any good thing from me.
>> Psalm 84:1-4, 10-11 (AMP)

When the sons of Korah sacrificed to God, it was more than a duty, it was their heart passion. As they approached the altar with burnt offerings they could see the smoke lazily ascending into Heaven from the burning sacrifices on the grate. It is here that they would again pray the Psalms.

> O send out Your light, the truth that shines,
>> Let Your light lead me to You,
>> Let it bring me to Your holy hill,

Then will I come to God, I come to the altar of God,

I come to God my exceeding joy,

I praise You with sacrifice, my God.

Psalm 43: 3-4 (AMP)

You will grow as a Christian as you apply these Psalms of intimacy to your life. You will learn about the attributes of God and from that you will experience the Person of God. Yes, *you can know God,* but just as important, *God can know you. Lord, teach me Yourself.*

The Psalms of the Sons of Korah

PSALM 42:   LONGING FOR GOD

PSALM 43:   HOPING IN GOD

PSALM 44:   A PRAYER FOR THE DISTRESSED

PSALM 45:   THE BEAUTY OF THE KING

PSALM 46:   OUR REFUGE AND STRENGTH IN GOD

PSALM 47:   CELEBRATING THE LORD GOD MOST HIGH

PSALM 48:   THE BEAUTY OF THE CITY OF ZION

PSALM 49:   DISCERNING REAL VALUE IN LIFE

PSALM 84:   ENJOYING THE HOUSE OF GOD

PSALM 85:   THE PRAYER OF THE RETURNED EXILES

PSALM 87:   ZION, THE CITY OF GOD

PSALM 88:   A LAMENT OVER AFFLICTION

PSALM 42

*A Prayer To Experience The Presence Of God**

As the young deer being chased will thirst for water,

So my soul longs for Your presence, O Lord.

I thirst for You, O God.

    When will You let me stand again in Your presence?

Day and night I have cried for You,

    While my enemies jeer, "Where is your God?"

I remember when I used to come to You,

    Now it breaks my heart that I can't come into Your house.

Because I remember coming to You with a crowd of worshippers,

       I was singing and giving You thanks;

       I was praising You with other worshippers.

Now I am discouraged in my soul,

    I am cut off from Your house.

Yet, in the future I will return to Your presence;

    I will come again to Your house to praise You.

Now I am depressed because I can't drink from Your fountains,

    Because I remember You sent us water from Mt. Hermon;

Where the head waters of the Jordan begins,

    And from Mizpah where Your presence first dwelt in the land.

I hear the waves roaring in the sea,

    And I want You to refresh me again.

So I must drink daily from Your love to me,

    I must worship You each night with songs and prayer.

Even when I can't come close to You in the temple,

    I feel lost in the darkness.

And my enemies laugh at my commitment to You,

    They taunt me, saying, "Where is your God?"

When I am discouraged in my soul

    And my spirit is sad,

I will worship You in my heart;

    Because You strengthen my confidence,

You are my Lord, and my God.

Amen

*Instructions by the sons of Korah.

PSALM 43

A Prayer For Hope When You Are Discouraged

O Lord, examine me carefully;
  Then tell the ungodly what You see.
Deliver me from my deceitful enemies,
  And don't let dishonest people trap me.
You are my strength, O God;
  Why have You not listened to me?
  Why am I hurting because of my enemies?

Give me the light of Your wisdom,
  So I can make good decisions.
Let Your light guide me into godliness,
  I need to come into Your presence.
I will come to the altar to confess my sin,
  Then I will happily come to You;
  And then I will joyfully sing Your praises.

But now I am miserable and lonely,
  Why am I so upset?
O God, my hope and encouragement is in You;
  I will continue to praise You,
  You are my health and my Savior.

Amen

PSALM 44

*A Prayer For God To Stop Allowing Our Enemies To Defeat Us**

O Lord, I heard with my own ears
  All the mighty works You did in the past.
How You drove out the heathen from the Holy Land,
  You were the One who defeated them.
Our fathers did not originally conquer the land by their strength,
  You allowed them to possess it.
You are my King, O God,
  You can give the promised land to us.
By Your power we will push the heathen out of the land,
  We will subdue them when they rise up against us.
We will not trust in arms for victory,
  But You will save us from our enemies.
We will boast in You all day long,
  We will praise Your name forever. Selah!

But You abandoned us and let them defeat us,
  You didn't fight with us against our enemies.
You let us run away from our enemies,
  And they plundered our possessions.
We were as defenseless as sheep,
  We were defeated and scattered.
We were sold out to our enemies,
  But You did not get anything out of it.
We were a reproach to our neighbors,
  Those around us were puzzled when we were defeated.
We were cursed by our enemies,
  And mocked by everyone else.

I don't understand what is happening,

    And I am embarrassed by our failure.

I don't know how to answer those who attack me,

    I don't have any reason to give them.

Every thing has gone bad for us,

    Yet we have not forgotten You;

    We have not stopped obeying You.

Our heart is not hardened against You,

    Nor have we quit following You.

Even though You let our enemies punish us

    And let the shadow of death fall over us,

We have not forgotten the power of Your name;

    Nor have we stretched out our hands to false gods.

Will You not examine us now

    And know the secrets of our hearts?

We are suffering all the time because of Your will,

    We are like sheep ready to be slaughtered.

Awake, don't sleep when we need You;

    Don't cast us off forever.

Don't hide Your face from us,

    And don't put our suffering out of Your mind.

Because our spirit is crushed,

    Our desire to live is gone.

Get up and come help us,

    And save us because You are merciful.

                        Amen

*Instructions by the sons of Korah.

PSALM 45

A Prayer Of Gratitude
*For A Good Political Ruler**

O Lord, I have been thinking of a good thing;
    I'm speaking of the things about Your King,
    My tongue is a ready writer to record them.
The King is fairer than the children of man,
    Grace pours from his lips;
    You have always blessed him, my God.
The King straps his sword on his hip,
    He rides gloriously and majestically.
He prospers because of his truth and meekness,
    His right hand will act swiftly.
He will pierce the heart of his enemies,
    The nations will be subdued by him.
He shall rule for You forever,
    His scepter is Your scepter.
He loves those who do the right thing,
    And hates those who do wickedly;
    Therefore You anoint him with the oil of gladness.
His clothes smell of myrrh and aloes,
    You rejoice in the influence of his palace.
The King can choose a wife from many honorable women,
    One is chosen Queen by your authority.
All women should consider it an honor,
    To leave their family to become part of his family.
Therefore, the King will choose one who is beautiful;
    We follow him because he is wise.
Many women will bring gifts to the wedding,
    The rich will also seek the King's favor.

The bride shall have inward character,
   Her sparkling dress is woven from pure gold.
Needlework sets off her flowing train,
   Her bridesmaids follow her down the aisle.
They rejoice as they enter the King's presence,
   The beautiful bridesmaids enhance the ceremony.
The King shall have many sons by her,
   They shall be princes in his kingdom.

Lord, Your name will be forever remembered;
   Your people will praise You forever.

Amen

*Instructions by the sons of Korah.

PSALM 46

*A Prayer That Anticipates God's Protection During The End Times Judgment**

God, You are my refuge and strength;
   You are present to help when I have trouble.
Therefore I will not be afraid when the earth crumbles,
   When the mountains are cast into the seas;
Though all the oceans roar with storms
   And the mountains shake with earthquakes. Selah!

I will rest safely beside Your river in Your city,
   In the holy place of Your Tabernacle.
Your city shall not be shaken,
   Because You are in the midst of it;
   You shall give it stability.

The heathen will be angry,

The kingdoms of mankind will be overthrown.

But when You speak the Word,

The earth will melt under Your judgment.

You, O Lord of hosts, will be with me;

You, the God of Jacob, will be my refuge. Selah!

All people will see Your mighty works,

They will behold how You judge the earth.

You will make all war cease,

When the earth comes to its end.

You will break all weapons,

You will destroy all attack vehicles.

I will be still in Your presence

So I can learn to know You intimately.

We who have followed Your principles

Will be vindicated in that day among the heathen.

You, O Lord of hosts, will be with us;

You, the God of Jacob, will be my refuge.

Amen

*A song of the sons of Korah.

PSALM 47

A Prayer Glorifying The Lord Who Rules The Earth

Lord, I clap my hands to show You my approval;

I shout praises to You for Your triumph.

For You, the Most High God, are awesome;
  You are the great King over the earth.

You subdue our enemies before us,
  Putting them under our control.
You choose where I shall live,
  Just as You loved Jacob in giving him the promised land. Selah!

Lord, You enter Your Temple with might shouts;
  You are glorified with trumpet blasts.
Everyone is singing praises to You,
  They are singing worship songs to You our King.

You are the King over all the earth,
  I understand why I am praising You.
Lord, You reign over all people;
  You sit upon a holy throne.

The rulers of all the nations are here,
  They join me in praising You, the God of Abraham.
All the earth's rulers get their authority from You,
  You are everywhere honored.

Amen

*A Psalm by the sons of Korah.

PSALM 48

A Prayer Of Thanksgiving For God's Protection Of Jerusalem

Lord, You are great in Your city,
  And I greatly praise You in Your holy mountain.

Jerusalem is beautiful sitting among the peaks,
  The whole earth wants to see it.
Built upon Mount Zion, the holy place,
  It is Your city, my great King.
Lord, You live in Jerusalem's Temple,
  Your people live in safety there.

The kings of the earth assemble their armies,
  They planned to attack the city.
But when they saw the city's defenses,
  They retreated, knowing they couldn't take it.
They were afraid to attack it,
  Like a woman fears her coming labor pains;
  Like mighty ships fear an approaching hurricane.

I have heard about Jerusalem's glory
  Now I have seen it with my eyes.
This is Your city, O Lord of hosts,
  You will keep it safe forever. Selah!
O God, I meditate on Your loving kindness,
  When I enter Your presence in the Temple.
Your name deserves recognition, O God,
  You should be praised from the ends of the earth;
  Because Your hand defends this city.

Let the inhabitants of Mount Zion rejoice,
  When You finish inspecting the city,
When You've walked around the city's defenses,
  After You finish counting the towers;
  And You have examined the fortified walls,
  And You've taken note of her palaces;
  So You can describe it to future generations.

For You, Lord, are our God forever,

You will look out for us until we die.

Amen

PSALM 49

*A Prayer About The Futility Of Money, Power, And Wisdom Without God**

Lord, everyone in the world should know this;

I want everyone to pay attention to what I say.

Everyone—upper class and lower class,

Rich and poor want to understand one thing;

What is the secret to life?

Yet everyone should know how simple the answer is.

I have heard many proverbs try to explain it,

And I've heard many write poems about it.

Because God is the answer, I am not afraid when troubles come,

Nor when my enemies attack me.

Some think the secret is to have a lot of money,

So they are confident their money will solve their problems.

Yet they can't redeem themselves from death,

Their money can't get God to ransom their soul.

Redemption does not come that way,

No one has enough money to buy their way into Heaven

Where they will live forever with God.

The wise person must also die,

Just like the dumb and ignorant;

They all leave their money to someone else.

Everyone thinks they will live forever,

And that their family name will endure forever;

So they attach their name to something special.

But even the respected person will die,

Just like all animals eventually die.

Those who think they'll never die are not smart,

But they will be remembered as a fool. Selah!

They are like sheep that will eventually be killed,

Death shall feed on them in the grave.

The godly will ultimately rule them,

They will lose their beauty in death.

But Lord, You will redeem me in the day of my death;

You will keep me from corruption. Selah!

So it doesn't bother me when wicked people get rich.

Nor do I care that they live in big expensive houses.

Because they can't take it with them when they die,

Their money can't help them in the grave.

They spent their money on themselves when they were alive,

They did everything to enhance their reputation.

They will die just like everyone else,

But they shall not see the light of Your presence.

These people who wrap themselves in money

Will die just like all the animals.

Amen

*A Psalm by the sons of Korah.

HOW TO PRAY

When You Need Deliverance: The Psalms Of Asaph

Asaph wrote twelve Psalms to reflect his fears and frustrations in life. These Asaph Psalms focus on how God intervened for him in difficult situations. Asaph was a priest of God who fled Jerusalem with David, the future King of Israel. Saul chased David all over the Judean hills trying to kill him. During these thirteen difficult years in exile, Asaph was chased with David. During the long cold nights sleeping on the hard ground, Asaph remembered the presence of God in the Temple, and he thanked God for preserving his life each time the enemy almost killed him. Many times Saul almost caught David and his company; and if Saul had captured them, he would have killed David and Asaph. So Asaph prayed Psalms of gratitude for God's constant deliverance.

Night after night Asaph was separated from friends and home. He might have wondered if he would ever be returned to the priesthood and the Temple. During these nights of solitude he prayed for God's intervention. "In the day of my trouble I sought the Lord . . . I complained, and my spirit was overwhelmed. And I said, 'This is my anguish; but I will remember the years of the right hand of the Most High.' I will also meditate on all Your work, and talk of Your deeds" (Ps. 77:2, 3, 10, 12). *Lord, thank You for protecting me when I cried to You in danger, and thank You for delivering me from danger I didn't know about.*

The Psalms Of Asaph

PSALM 50: GOD HIMSELF IS JUDGE

PSALM 73: PRAYER FOR FORGIVENESS

A day came when David was elevated king over Judah, and seven years later he became king over all twelve tribes of Israel. In that day Asaph again entered into the presence of God in the Temple. Again Asaph worshipped God for allowing him to return to the holy hill of Zion.

For promotion comes neither from the east,
　Nor from the west,
God is the all-knowing Judge,
　God puts one down,
　God puts another up.
In God's hand is a cup, He pours the same on all,
　The wicked drinks, and is cut off,
　The righteous drinks, and is exalted.
　　Psalm 75: 6-8 (author's translation)

However, even when Asaph slept again in the Temple, he sang Psalms about those cold, lonely nights in the open fields, where he was separated from his family and the Temple of God. It is here that he prayed:

I remember in times of trouble, my songs in the night,
　I prayed constantly to the Lord,
　Will You cast me away forever,

Is Your mercy gone forever?

I remember in infirmity, God's right hand protected me,

I remembered His past wonders,

I meditated all night on His works.

Psalm 77:6-7, 10-11 (author's translation)

Asaph is called the chief musician by David and by Solomon. The sons of Asaph continued to serve after he died (see 2 Chron. 35:15). Some historians believe the sons of Asaph continued into and through the exile (see Ps. 74, 79, 81, 83). These Psalms could have been prayed by the sons of Asaph during the Babylonian captivity. A few others think that Asaph might have written these Psalms by prophecy. Perhaps these Psalms expressed his experiences when he and David were exiled from Jerusalem, but were predictive of the nation's exile from the Promised Land.

When you begin to pray the Psalms of Asaph, remember how God has delivered you in the past. How God has protected you in the past is predictive of how God will deliver you in the future. Pray with Asaph, "I have considered the days of old, the years of ancient times. I call to remembrance my song in the night; I meditate within my heart, and my spirit makes diligent search'" (Ps. 77:5-6).

When you remember what God has done in the past, it can take away fear of the future, or discouragement in the present. Asaph prayed, "'This is my anguish; but I will remember the years of the right hand of the Most High.' I will remember the works of the Lord; surely I will remember Your wonders of old. I will also meditate on all Your work, and talk of Your deeds" (Ps. 77:10-12).

The answered prayers of Asaph are motivation for others to pray, "That they may set their hope in God, and not forget the works of God, but keep His commandments" (Ps. 78:7). Maybe you don't understand what God is doing in your life. Then pray the Psalms of Asaph. Why? Because Asaph had trouble understanding what was happening in his life. "Until I went into the sanctuary of God; then I understood their end" (Ps. 73:17). *Lord, show me the light at the end of the tunnel.*

Asaph Prayers For You

Lord, help me never get so discouraged that I will forget what You have done in the past, and forget to trust You for what You can do in the present.

Lord, help me to understand what You are doing so that I may turn defeat into victory, and that I may see Your hand working in my life.

Lord, may I apply, in the light of this present day, what I have learned in the dark night of desperation.

Lord, may I help people who have difficulty understanding how You can help them, by sharing with them how You helped me in the past.

Amen

PSALM 50

*A Prayer—Recognizing God Will Judge Everyone By Their Heart Attitude**

O Lord, my mighty God, You have spoken;
> You have called everyone from one end of the earth to the other.
Out of beautiful Mount Zion where You live,
> Your glorious radiance is shining.

You are not silent about what's coming,
> A fire will burn away everything that is hidden.
Heaven and earth will really see how everything comes out,
> As You judge Your people. Selah!

You will gather everyone in Your presence,
> Even those who made a covenant to worship You.
Then the Heavens will testify if they were obedient,
> Then You will reveal everything in their hearts.

O Lord, You call Your people to listen;
> As You bring charges against them,
> You are the Lord, their God.
Lord, You know Your people have sacrificed;
> They continually brought burnt offerings to You.
But You don't need their animals;

Because all the cattle on a thousand hills are Yours,
You know all the birds of the air,
All living creatures in the earth belong to You.

If You needed meat for satisfaction,
    You wouldn't need people to bring it to You.
Because the earth is Yours and everything in it,
    You don't need the animals that Your people sacrifice;
    And You don't need the blood offerings they bring.
What You want is the gratitude of thankful hearts,
    You want Your people to do what they promised You.
You want them to trust You in the day of trouble,
    You want them to glorify You.

But You tell the disobedient,
    Don't pretend You obey me by reciting my laws.
Because they refuse to love Your ways,
    They never pay attention to what You want.
When they saw a thief, they helped him,
    And they got involved in adultery.
They repeated all the evil things they heard,
    And they lied when confronted with their actions.
They accused others of the evil they did,
    They even lied about their brothers.

Lord, You kept silent while they did these things;
    And they thought You didn't care.
Now You are calling them to account for their actions,
    Now You are looking at their crimes.
They must realize they have ignored You,
    They must realize You can tear them into pieces;
    And no one will be able to help them.

You are pleased with grateful hearts that accompany sacrifices,

    You accept those who worship You honestly;

    These are the ones You save.

Amen

*A Psalm of Asaph.

HOW TO PRAY

When You Need Forgiveness: Psalm 51

When you feel guilty, nothing feels better than God's forgiveness. David asked God, "Hide Your face from my sins, and blot out all my iniquities" (Ps. 51:9). *Lord, I want to feel clean. Forgive me.*

It doesn't make any difference what you've done. Sometimes a small sin will rip your soul apart, especially if it's something you can't quit. Then the small sin gets bigger. When you feel terrible—small sin or big sin—you still feel like you'll die. What should you do? Begin where you feel worse, begin with your sin. "I acknowledge my transgressions, and my sin is always before me" (Ps. 51:3). *Lord, I see my sin laughing at me; I acknowledge I did it.*

Right now your cup is empty, all your goodness is gone. You feel like you've poured out milk and filled your cup with garbage. "Have mercy upon me, O God" (Ps. 51:1). Isn't that what you need, God's mercy? *Lord, don't condemn me now.* Also you need your cup cleansed. "According to the multitude of Your tender mercies, blot out my transgressions" (Ps. 51:1). *Lord, I'm holding my cup out to You.*

Yes, that's what you need more than anything else—purity. "Cleanse me from my sin, so I can be clean, wash me so I can be whiter than snow" (Ps. 51:7, PTP).

When you feel bad, you want some happiness in your life. You want the peace you had before you sinned. "Restore unto me the joy of Your salvation, and give me a new spirit to obey You" (Ps. 51:12, PTP). *Lord, I want to be happy again.*

When your sin oppresses, you feel God will never use you again. You think that you'll never be able to serve God again. But with forgiveness comes restoration to service. "Do not cast me away from Your presence, and do not take Your Holy Spirit from me. Then I will teach transgressors Your ways" (Ps. 51:11, 13). *Lord I want to serve You. Use me.*

PSALM 51

*A Prayer—Seeking Restoration To Fellowship With God After You Sin**

Lord, have mercy on me according to Your loving nature;
    Because of Your mercy blot out my transgressions.
Wash me completely from my sin,
    So I will be clean of my guilt.
For I acknowledge my terrible deed,
    I cannot get it out of my mind.
Against You and no one else have I sinned,
    In doing what was evil in Your sight.
You are absolutely right to convict me,
    And Your punishment is just.

I was born a sinner,
    And I have sinned since the beginning.
But You want us to be inwardly truthful,
    Because that is where You communicate with us.
Cleanse me from my sins so I can be clean,
    Wash me so I can be whiter than snow.
I want to be happy like I was before,
    I want my broken spirit to rejoice again.
Hide my sin from Your face,
    Cleanse my guilty conscience from guilt.
O God, create in me a clean heart,
    And renew a right spirit in me.
Don't kick me out of Your presence,

And don't take Your Holy Spirit from me.

Restore to me the joy of Your salvation,

And give me a new spirit to obey You.

Then I will tell sinners how to be saved,

And they will turn to You.

Amen

*A Psalm of David, when Nathan the prophet came unto him, after he had gone in to Bathsheba.

PSALM 52

*A Prayer That Recognizes God's Judgment On Liars, But His Care For His People**

Lord, the wicked boast about their sin;

But Your grace, O God, continues to endure.

They continue to think up more evil,

Their deceitful tongue cuts me to the core.

They love disobedience more than obedience,

And they would rather lie than tell the truth. Selah!

They get great pleasure out of hurting people with their lies,

Their tongue naturally lies all the time.

But You, O Lord, will destroy lying people,

You will separate them from Your presence;

And they will not receive eternal life. Selah!

Your followers will see what You do,

And they will be astonished at Your actions

When You judge those who hide behind their sin;

Because they do not obey You.

But Lord, I am just a small plant;

  Growing in Your house.

I trust in Your continuing love,

  That takes care of me forever and ever.

I will worship You eternally,

  Because of what You have done for me.

I will seek the intimacy of Your presence,

  Which You give to those who seek You.

                                    Amen

*A Psalm of instruction by David, when Doeg the Edomite came and told Saul, and said unto him, David is come to the house of Abimelech.

PSALM 53

*A Prayer Thanking God For Delivering His People And Judging Sinners**

Lord, only fools say You don't exist;

  They say that because of their corruption,

  There is none that do good.

Lord, You look down from Heaven

  To see if anyone has spiritual understanding;

  To see if anyone is seeking You.

But no one is turning from sin to You,

  Sin has corrupted their thinking;

  There is none that do good.

Lord, don't sinners understand their sin?

  They never call upon You.

You will terrorize them like never before,

  When You judge them for their sin;

  Because they have despised You.

Lord, send salvation to rescue Your people Israel;

Bring them back to Jerusalem from captivity,

Then they will shout for joy.

Amen

*A Psalm of instruction by David.

PSALM 54

*A Prayer Of Deliverance From Your Enemies And God's Judgment On Them**

Lord, I need You to come deliver me,

And vindicate me by Your power.

Listen to my petitions

And give me the things I ask.

Because strangers are out to get me,

They are trying to destroy me;

They don't care about Your rule. Selah!

Lord, You have delivered me in the past,

By helping those who helped me.

Let my enemies suffer the evil things they plan for me,

Judge them by Your Word.

Then I will freely sacrifice to You,

I will praise You for Your goodness to me;

Because You will deliver me from trouble,

And I will see my enemies defeated.

Amen

*A Psalm of instruction by David, when the Ziphims came and said to Saul, Does not David hide himself with us?

PSALM 55

*A Prayer For God To Destroy An Enemy Who Used To Be A Friend**

Lord, hear my prayer that I speak to You;
    Don't hide Yourself from my supplication.
Come hear the request I make,
    I am agonizing over this matter.
My enemy has spoken against me,
    He is putting immense pressure on me;
    Accusing me of committing sin.

My heart aches over this matter,
    And I am scared to death.
I tremble all over out of fear,
    Because I feel like I'm going to die.

O Lord, I wish I had wings like a bird;
    I would fly away from this problem.
And would flee away into the forest,
    I would quickly get away from this trouble;
    There I would rest from this storm. Selah!

O Lord, destroy my enemy because of what he's saying;
    He's stirring up hatred and violence around me.
Day and night he goes about spreading rumors,
    Stirring up strife everywhere he goes.
He is motivated by his sin,
    Then he covers it up with lies and deceit.

If my trouble came from an outside enemy,

I could deal with it better.
But it didn't come from someone who hated me,
   Because then I could have handled the issue.
But my trouble comes from an insider,
   A person that I thought was my friend.
I had opened up my heart to this friend,
   We went together to worship You.
Lord, I pray that he dies
   And is quickly buried out of my sight;
   So he won't stir up any more trouble.

As for me, I will call upon You, O Lord;
   Because I know You will save me.
I will pray to You, evening, morning and noon,
   Because I know You will hear me.
You have given me peace about this trouble,
   Even though there are many against me.

Lord, I have a specific request to make;
   Make my enemy suffer the affliction I've had. Selah!
He doesn't fear You or Your punishment,
   Because he hasn't been convicted of his sin.
My enemy attacks Your people who have treated him kindly,
   He has violated every law of decency.
The words of my enemy were as smooth as butter,
   But he planned in his heart to kill me.
His words were as silky as oil,
   Yet he planned to knife me in the back.

Lord, I cast my burdens upon You;
   Because I know You will sustain me,
   You will never permit the righteous to be destroyed.

Lord, destroy my enemy and kill him;

> Don't let him live out his life,

> I will trust You to do this request.

Amen

*A Psalm of instruction by David.

PSALM 56

*A Prayer For Protection From A Particular Enemy**

O Lord, be merciful to me in danger;

> Because my enemy would destroy me,

> He daily oppresses me.

My enemy is constantly trying to kill me,

> There are many that oppose me, O Lord Most High.

When I am most afraid,

> I will trust in Your protection.

I will exalt Your Word

> Because that will protect me,

> I will not be afraid of what my enemy can do.

Every day he twists my words,

> Using every thing against me.

My enemy gets others to help him,

> He sneaks around behind my back;

> Looking for ways to destroy me.

Lord, don't let him get away with his sin;

> Judge him by Your wrath.

Lord, You know I meditate on You;

> Don't forget my tears over this matter.

When I cried to You, my enemies were stopped;
    Therefore I know You are for me.
I have trusted You for protection,
    I will not be afraid of what they can do to me.

O Lord, this is what I promise to do;
    I will praise You for safety.
Because You have protected me from destruction,
    You kept the evil one from me;
    You helped me walk before You in this life.

Amen

*A Psalm carved on stone by David, when the Philistines took him in Gath.

PSALM 57

A Prayer To Glorify God When Enemies Attack

Have mercy on me, O Lord, have mercy;
    I trust You to protect me.
I'll hide in the shadow of Your wing
    Until my troubles pass by.
I cry unto You, O God, Most High;
    Because You fulfill Your plan for me.
You sent help from Heaven to save me
    From my enemy that would destroy me. Selah!
    You showed me Your love and faithfulness.

I am surrounded by hungry lions,
    And lie among a dangerous enemy.
Their teeth are piercing like spears,
    Their tongues are sharp as a sword.
O God, You are exalted above the Heavens,

Your glory shines over all the earth.

My enemy prepared a trap for me,

   And I am discouraged by this pressure.

He dug a hole for me to fall in,

   But he has fallen into it himself. Selah!

I will be faithful to You, O God;

   I will faithfully praise and worship You.

I will wake up early to praise You,

   I will praise You with harp and song.

I will praise You among the unsaved,

   I will praise You among the believers.

Because Your love reaches to the heavens,

   Your faithfulness extends to the clouds.

I exalt You, O God, above the heavens,

   Let Your glory flow over all the earth.

Amen

*A Psalm carved on stone by David, when he fled from Saul in the cave.

PSALM 58

*A Prayer For Destruction Of Your Enemies When They Are About To Win**

Lord, deliver me from my enemies;

   Defend me from those who attack me.

Deliver me from those who do iniquity,

   Protect me from vicious people.

They are waiting to pounce on me

   And they are strong enough to destroy me.

They are not trying to punish me for my sin,
  Nor are they judging my sin.

They are not concerned with my faults,
  O Lord, come defend me.
Lord, You are the God of the fighting angels,
  O Lord, come defeat the ungodly;
  Do not let them go unpunished.

They sneak around after dark,
  They bark like a dog to scare me.
They make strange sounds with their mouth,
  And they think no one hears them.

They tell others about their intent to kill me,
  And they think that no one knows.
But O Lord, You will laugh at them,
  You will confuse the ungodly.

Because my enemy is strong,
  I look to You for my defense.
You, O Lord, will go before me in mercy,
  You will let me see my enemies punished.

If you kill the evil man quickly,
  The godly will get complacent.
So scatter them now by Your power;
  And punish them slowly, O Lord, my protector.

My enemies sin with the words of their mouth,
  They angrily boast and curse.
Show them Your anger in judgment,
  So they realize the God of Jacob rules this earth.

Let them whine like a whipped dog,

That roams homelessly the streets of the city;

Scavenging for food in the garbage,

And never have the satisfaction of a good meal.

I will sing loudly about Your power,

In the morning everyone will hear me sing of Your mercy.

Because You have defended me from danger,

I have found safety from trouble in You.

I sing unto You, O my Defense,

You are my defense, O God of mercy.

Amen

*A Psalm carved on stone by David.

PSALM 59

A Prayer To Defeat Your Enemies
*And Praise When God Does It**

Deliver me from my enemies, O God;

Protect me from those who attack me.

Deliver me from those who rebel against You,

And save me from murderers.

They are planning to ambush me,

These violent men are waiting for me;

Even though I've done nothing to them.

I am innocent, yet they seek to kill me;

Come see my dilemma and help me.

O Lord God Almighty, God of Israel;
    Rise up to punish the lawless,
    Don't show them any mercy. Selah!

They come prowling around at evening,
    Snarling like hungry dogs.
They belch out threatening words of harm,
    And they think no one can hurt them.

But You laugh at them, Lord,
    You scoff at the godless heathen.
I wait for You because You are my strength,
    O God, You are my defense.

O loving God, come to help me;
    Let me triumph over my enemies.
But don't kill them instantly, O Lord;
    Scatter them from Your presence,
    And punish them slowly, O Lord my shield.

Because they say filthy things,
    They curse and lie with their mouth;
    Let their words condemn them.
Destroy them in Your anger,
    Consume them completely;
    That everyone will realize You rule in Israel. Selah!

My enemies come prowling around at evening,
    Snarling like hungry dogs.
Let them scavenge for something to eat,
    And bark when they go hungry.

But I will sing of Your power,

> Every morning I will sing of Your love.

You have defended me from my enemies,

> You protect me in time of trouble.

I sing to You, O my Strength;

> You protect me, O my loving God.

Amen

*A Psalm carved on stone by David; when Saul sent men, and they watched the house to kill him.

PSALM 60

*A Prayer For God To Return And Help Fight Your Enemies**

O God, why have You not helped me;

> Why have You let my enemy defeat me?

Are You angry with something I have done?

> Come back to me and help me.

You have shaken the ground under my feet,

> Now come give me a solid place to stand on.

You have given me a hard time,

> You have made me drink bitter water.

But we who fear You can rally to Your banner,

> It is displayed because of Your truth, Selah!

Save me with Your strong right hand,

> That I may be delivered.

You have spoken from Your sanctuary,

I will rejoice in Your decisions.

You have divided to Your people,
   The inheritance that is appropriate for them.
   Shechem, the valley of Succoth, Gilead,
   And Manasseh, Ephraim, and Judah.
You rejected Moab as dirty water,
   Edom and Philistia You stepped upon.

Lord, I need someone to bring me;
   Into Your fortified city of Jerusalem,
   To help me defeat Your enemies.
O God, will You again be my helper;
   Even though You rejected me in the past?
   Even though You stopped fighting for me?

Please help me defeat my enemies,
   Because the help of man is not enough.
Only through You will I be victorious, O God;
   For You can trample down my enemies.

Amen

*A Psalm carved on stone by David, to teach; when he strove with Aram-naharaim and with Aram-zobah, and Joab returned, and smote twelve thousand of Edom in the valley of salt.

PSALM 61

A Prayer For Deliverance From Your Enemies And Blessings On Your Leader

O God, hear me when I cry to You,
   Listen to me when I pray.
I will cry to You from the ends of the earth,

For my heart is heavy burdened.
Lead me to the Rock that is higher than I,
Because You won't let my enemies reach me there.
I want to live forever in Your Tabernacle,
Your wings will protect me from danger. Selah!

You have listened to my vows,
You have given me an inheritance;
The same one You give to all who fear Your name.
Give a long life to the king,
May his reign reach across generations.
Bless Your people through his rule,
And watch over him in Your love and faithfulness.
Then I will sing praises unto Your name,
And I will perform my vows each day.

Amen

*A Psalm of David.

PSALM 62

*A Prayer For God To Protect You When Your Enemies Have The Upper Hand**

Lord, I wait for You to give me rest;
My salvation comes from You.
You only are my rock and salvation,
You are my fortress when I am shaken.

I have so many enemies,
They are all trying to destroy me.
They think I'm a sagging fence
That's about to fall down.

They intend to knock me down,

    They tell lies about me.

They bless me to my face,

    But in their heart they curse me. Selah!

O God, I find my rest in You;

    My hope is only in You.

You alone are my rock and salvation,

    You only are my fortress where I am secure.

My salvation and hope come from You,

    Hide me in a rock where I will be safe.

Lord, I trust in You at all times;

    I pour out my heart to You,

    Because You are my refuge. Selah!

Lord, I know lower class people are just steam;

    And higher class people only put on a show.

When I weigh them in the balance,

    All people are nothing more than a breath.

I will not trust in money from extortion,

    Nor security I can get by stealing from people.

Even though everyone else is getting rich,

    Money will not be the purpose of my life.

I have heard You speak once to me,

    You don't have to tell me again;

    That You have all power.

O Lord, You never stop loving me;

You will reward all people,

According to what they deserve.

Amen

*A Psalm of David.

PSALM 63

*A Prayer Of Rejoicing Because You Have Worshipped God**

O God, You are my God;

Early each morning I will search for You.

Because my soul thirsts for You,

Everything in me yearns for You.

As someone searching for water in a desert,

Where there is none;

I have seen You in the sanctuary,

I felt Your power and glory.

I continually praise You,

Because of Your love to me.

I will bless You as long as I live,

Lifting up my hands to You in worship.

You satisfy me more than money or food,

I will praise You from a joyful heart.

I will meditate on You lying in my bed,

And think about You all night long.

Because You have helped me in many ways,

I rejoice in the shadow of Your wings.

I will walk close beside You,

Your strong right hand will steady me.

But those that scheme to destroy me,

   Will die and be buried.

They will die by the sword,

   And scavengers will eat their remains.

But the king shall rejoice in God,

   And those who are loyal to him will rejoice;

   While liars will be gagged.

Amen

*A Psalm of David, when he was in the wilderness of Judah.

PSALM 64

A Prayer For Victory Against Your Enemies

O God, listen to my request;

   Don't let my enemies terrify me.

Don't let their conspiracy succeed,

   Protect me from their rebellion.

They sharpen their tongue like a sword,

   They aim cutting words at me like an arrow.

They shout at the innocent with their accusations,

   Never considering consequences or reprisals.

My enemies encourage each other to attack me,

   They plan together their deceptive snares;

   They think no one will know.

They devise a cunning trap for me,

   Using their creative mind and evil heart;

   Thinking it is a perfect plan.

But You, Lord, will shoot arrows at them;
  Suddenly, they shall be wounded.
Their lies will be turned against them,
  And all their supporters will abandon them.

Everyone will then fear You, my God,
  Because they will realize what You have done.
The righteous will rejoice in You,
  And Your people will praise You.

Amen

*A Psalm of David.

PSALM 65

*A Prayer Of Praise For God's Presence In Zion And His Physical Provision**

O Lord, I can't wait till I get to Zion to praise You;
  I will keep my vows unto You.
Because You have heard our prayers,
  Everyone will come to You.

My heart seems overwhelmed with sin,
  But You continually forgive me.
Those chosen by You are blessed,
  They come into Your presence;
  They dwell in Your courts.
They shall be satisfied with Your goodness,
  Even living in Your holy Temple.

You have answered our prayers with wonderful things,
    You are the God of my salvation.
You are the source of my confidence,
    You are the assurance of those far off.

By Your mighty strength You created the mountains,
    You have clothed Yourself with all power.
You silenced the roaring waves of the seas,
    You quieted the rebellious heathen.

Those who live at the ends of the earth fear You,
    There is rejoicing at the place where the sun rises and sets.
You send rain to make the earth fertile,
    The rivers of God will always have water
    To give us a harvest of grain.

You send rain upon our ploughed fields,
    The rows are damp with showers;
    Every spring You bless us with new growth.
You crown the farming year with good crops,
    You walk in our fields to give us a harvest.

The wilderness grows good things for us,
    The rolling hills rejoice to give us food.
The pastures are filled with flocks of animals,
    The valleys are covered with corn;
    All growing things sing for joy.

                                        Amen

*A Psalm and song of David.

PSALM 66

A Prayer Of Thanksgiving
*For God's Forgiveness And Provision**

O God, I joyfully shout praises to You;

    I join other people in happy praise.

I sing loudly to honor Your name,

    Making my praises to You glorious.

O God, Your works are powerfully awesome;

    So that Your enemies recognize You.

All the earth shall worship You,

    And sing unto Your name. Selah!

Let everyone come see Your awesome works,

    What You are doing for the children of mankind.

You turned the Red Sea to dry land,

    Your children walked through it on foot;

    They rejoiced in You every step of the way.

You will always rule by Your power,

    You see everything the nations do;

    Don't let the rebellious exalt themselves. Selah!

Everyone blesses You, O my God;

    Hear the voice of their praise.

Our lives are in Your hands,

    Because You keep our feet from straying.

You have examined us thoroughly,

    You have purified us as silver is refined.

You have caught us in Your net,

    And made us serve You as prisoners.

You allowed the enemy to ride rough shod over us,

You allowed us to be tested with fire and water;
But You brought us out into a wealthy place.

Now I come into Your presence with sacrifices,
I will fulfill all the vows I made to You.
Those promises I made publicly to You
When I was going through difficulties.
Now I offer to You sacrifices of praise,
I will give You everything I have;
I will worship You with the best of my life. Selah!
Let all who fear You, come to hear about Your goodness;
I will tell them what You did for me.

I cried to You for help,
My cry was really worship to You.
If my thoughts were motivated by sin,
You would not have heard me.
But You did hear me when I cried,
You listened to my request.
I praise You for not neglecting my prayer,
Nor did You quit loving me.

Amen

*A song or Psalm.

PSALM 67

*A Prayer For The Coming Kingdom Of Prosperity**

God, be merciful to us and bless us;
Let Your face shine on us. Selah!
So Your way may be known upon earth,
And Your prosperity known by all people.

Then all people will worship You with praise,
  Yes, all people will worship You.
Then all people will be glad and joyfully sing,
  Because You will examine everyone correctly;
  And rule them properly. Selah!

Then all people will worship You with praise,
  Yes, all people will worship You.
Then the earth will have a great harvest,
  And You will bless us with Your presence;
Yes, You will bless us with Your presence.
  And everyone will reverently trust You.

Amen

*A Psalm or song.

PSALM 68

*A Prayer Of Praise For God's Final Victory Over His Enemies**

Arise, O God, scatter Your enemies;
  Chase everyone that hates You.
As smoke is driven by the wind,
  Chase Your enemies away.
As wax is melted by the fire,
  Let Your presence judge them.
May Your children rejoice in Your presence,
  Let them rejoice exceedingly.

I sing praises to You, O God;
  I magnify You that rideth the Heavens;
  I rejoice in Your name, Jehovah.

God, You are a father to the fatherless;
 You are a protective judge to widows.
You give us all a family,
 You set the captive free;
 But You punish the rebellious.
O God, when You led us into the wilderness
 You marched victoriously before us. Selah!

The earth shook at Your presence,
 You caused an earthquake on Mount Sinai.
You sent a refreshing rain when Your people were weary,
 You confirmed that they were Your inheritance.
Your people lived by Your goodness,
 You took care of the poor who couldn't care for themselves.
You gave us Your Word,
 Your people were eager to tell others what You said.

Kings of armies ran from You,
 There was plenty of spoil for the families.
Though Your people were poor and hungry,
 You gave them birds to eat;
 They were satisfied as if they had silver and gold.
When You came scattering manna for them to eat,
 The ground was as white as snow.
The hill in which You have chosen to dwell,
 Is exalted above all mountains.

You have chosen to dwell on earth forever.
 All the hills will leap for joy,
You are surrounded by unnumbered chariots and angels,
 As You were surrounded by glory on Mount Sinai.
You ascended to Your eternal home on high,

You led a parade of captives.
You received gifts from Your people,
   And from those who rebelled against You;
   Now You will live among us.

We bless You, our Lord of salvation;
   Because You daily load us with good things. Selah!
You are the God of salvation,
   You rescue me from death.
You will shatter the heads of Your enemies,
   Wounding them because of their continual trespasses.
You will gather them into judgment,
   You will bring them from the depths of the sea,
   That You may punish them completely;
   And those that belong to You will taste victory.

We will see Your victory parade,
   You will march triumphantly into Your sanctuary.
The singers will go before You followed by musicians,
   With young girls playing tambourines.
Praise to You from Your people,
   Praises to You in Your sanctuary.
The small tribe of Benjamin enters with its leaders,
   Followed by the leaders of Judah, Zebulun, and Napthali.

God, summon Your power to display Your strength;
   Just as You did it in the past.
Kings will bring gifts to You
   Unto Your presence in the temple of Jerusalem.
Find Your enemies that hide from You,
   Those that flee to the farthest places on earth;
   That they may recognize Your authority over them.

Leaders from Egypt will bow to You,
   The leaders in Ethiopia will recognize You.

The kingdoms of the earth will sing to You. Selah!
   They will sing praises to You.
To You, who rides on the highest Heaven;
   To You, who thunders with Your voice.
All proclaim Your power, O God;
   All recognize Your majesty over Israel,
   And Your strength in the skies.
You are awesome in Your sanctuary,
   You give power and strength to Your people.

Praise to You, O God.

                                        Amen

*A Psalm or song of David.

PSALM 69

*A Prayer For God To Save You From Trouble And Condemn Your Persecutors**

Save me, O God, from the waters of trouble;
   They are about to flow over my head.
I am sinking in the mud of problems,
   There is no solid ground to stand upon.
I have fallen into dangerous water,
   And I am about to drown.
I am exhausted from yelling for help,
   My voice is gone and my eyes are swollen from crying;
   I'm waiting for You to save me.

I have more enemies than hairs on my head,

    They don't have any reason to destroy me;

    They make me give back what I didn't steal.

Lord, You know my weaknesses;

    I can't hide my sins from You.

May Your children not be embarrassed by me,

    O Lord, You are God of the fighting angels;

    May I not be a hindrance to those seeking You.

I put up with sarcasm for Your sake,

    And have lost my self-esteem.

My friends don't even claim to know me,

    And my relatives turn their backs on me.

My greatest desire is to be in Your house,

    And those who would insult You, insult me instead.

They laugh at me when I fast to seek You,

    They make fun of me when I prepare for prayer.

The leaders continually ridicule my faith,

    And the drunks make me the butt of their jokes.

But, I continue to pray to You, O Lord;

    Knowing You will eventually listen to me.

In Your great mercy hear me,

    And save me from all of my troubles.

Deliver me from being stuck in the mud,

    Do not let me sink any further.

Deliver me from those who hate me,

    And for the deep waters of trouble.

Don't let circumstances overwhelm me,

    Nor allow death to swallow me up.

Answer my cry to You, O Lord;
　　According to the goodness of Your love.
Don't turn Your face from me,
　　Quickly, come help me with my troubles.
Come help me through these difficulties,
　　Deliver me from my enemies.

You know the insults I endure,
　　You know what my enemies have said.
Their accusations have insulted me,
　　And broken my spirit.
I looked for someone to help me,
　　But no one seemed to care.
Instead, I got more sarcasm;
　　And they continued to criticize me.

May their food turn sour in their stomach,
　　And let them feel the anguish they heap on me.
May they be blinded by their sin,
　　And may they be too weak to do anything.

Pour Your anger on them,
　　And punish them for what they've done.
Let their homes be like a mortuary,
　　And may no one live with them.
Because they mock those You are correcting,
　　They add pain to those You discipline.
Search carefully to find everyone of their sins,
　　Don't let them enjoy Your forgiveness,
Blot their families out of the book of life,
　　And not be listed with Your followers.

I am suffering from much pain,

    Deliver me to solid ground.

I will sing praises to Your name,

    I will magnify You with thanksgiving.

May the results of my suffering please You,

    More than the sacrifice of an animal.

The humble will recognize what You are doing,

    Those who seek You will live better lives.

Because You hear those who seek You,

    You do not despise Your followers.

Lord, be praised by the heavens and earth;

    Be magnified by the seas, and their inhabitants.

God save Mount Zion, and rebuild the cities of Judah;

    Your people will live securely in Your land.

The children of Your followers will inherit it,

    And those who love You will live there forever.

                            Amen

*A Psalm of David.

PSALM 70

*A Prayer For God To Come Quickly To Help You**

Come quickly, Lord, save me;

    I need Your help now.

Confuse and embarrass those who want to destroy me,

    Reverse their plots against me.

Give them what they plan for me;

    Because they laugh and sneer at me.

Let those who seek Your protection,
    Find joy in Your presence.
Let those who love Your salvation,
    Continually magnify You.
But I am poor and needy,
    Come quickly, O God, help me.
You are my deliverer, O Lord;
    Don't tarry along the way.

Amen

*A Psalm of remembrance by David.

PSALM 71

A Prayer For Continued Protection In Old Age When You Can't Protect Yourself

Lord, I put my trust in You;
    Don't let me be embarrassed.
Do the right thing by delivering me from my enemies,
    Hear me and save me.
Let me hide in You,
    Where I can always find protection.
Give the order to save me,
    Because You are my rock and defense.

O God, deliver me from the evil one;
    From the grasp of evil persecutors.
Lord God, You are my hope;
    I've trusted You since childhood.
You have protected me from birth,
    Since I came from my mother's womb;
    Therefore, I've always praised You.

I've become a role model to many,
>   Because You have been my strength and defense.
I tell everyone of Your splendid grace,
>   I praise You all the time.
Don't turn Your back on me when I'm old,
>   Don't forsake me when my energy is gone.
I have enemies who conspire against me,
>   They want to destroy me.
My enemies think You're finished with me,
>   So they are coming to get me;
>   Thinking no one will help me.
O God, come help me now;
>   I need You right away.
Embarrass my enemies because of their treachery,
>   Let them suffer what they plan for me.

I will always trust You,
>   I will praise You more and more.
I will always have hope,
>   I will praise You as long as I live.
I will talk all day of Your righteousness,
>   It is more than I can measure.
I will go on in Your strength, O Lord God;
>   I will testify only about You and Your righteousness.
You have been my teacher since I was a youth,
>   To this day I tell everyone of Your marvelous works.
Do not forsake me now that I'm old and gray-headed,
>   Let me tell the next generation about Your power;
>   So those growing up know Your miracles.

Your righteousness is superb, O God;
>   You have done wonderful things that others couldn't do.

You have allowed me to suffer many ways,
But You will resurrect me from the grave;
You will restore my life to me.
You will again honor me in the future,
And comfort me with Your kindness.
I will praise You with my harp,
Because of Your faithfulness.
I will sing praises to You with my harp,
Because You are the Holy One of Israel.
I will shout loudly and sing for joy,
Because You have redeemed me.
I will tell everyone of Your righteousness,
Because You confounded my enemies.

Amen

PSALM 72

A Prayer For The Millennial Kingdom To Come And For Jesus To Rule The Earth*

O God, give Your wisdom to King David;
Give Your righteousness to his Son, Jesus.
He will rightly rule Your people,
He will make right decisions concerning them.
The mountains will enjoy peace,
The people will enjoy righteousness on the hills.
He will be favorable to the poor,
He will save the children of the needy;
He will destroy the enemy.
They will reverence Him from one generation to another,
As long as the sun and moon endure.
He shall bless them as rain on the grass,

As showers that water the earth.
The righteous will flourish under Him,
    There will be peace as long as the moon endures.
He shall rule from sea to sea,
    From the Jordan River to the ends of the earth.
Those who live in the wilderness will worship Him,
    His enemies will be defeated.
The foreign kings will recognize Him,
    Kings from Africa will give Him presents.
All kings will bow in worship before Him,
    All peoples will serve Him.
He will deliver the needy from trouble,
    And help the poor out of their calamity.
He will give to the needy,
    And He will reward the poor.
He will save them from death,
    Their life will be precious to Him.
He will receive gold from Africa,
    People will pray for Him continually;
    Daily they will praise Him.
In the coming day of prosperity,
    Corn shall grow everywhere.
Fruit will be available everywhere,
    And the cities will flourish.

His name, Jesus, will endure forever;
    It will continue as long as the sun.
And people will bless Him,
    All nations will call Him blessed.
Blessed are You, Lord God of Israel;
    Because You only do wonderful things.
Blessed be the glorious name of Jesus,

Let the whole earth be filled with His glory;

Amen and amen.

This ends the prayer of David, the son of Jesse.

Amen

*A Psalm for Solomon.

PSALM 73

A Prayer That Recognizes God Will Reward You For
Faithfulness And Punish The Ungodly For Their Rebellion*

God, You are truly good to Israel;

To those whose hearts are pure.

But I almost gave up my faith;

I came close to stumbling.

I wanted what selfish people had,

Especially when I saw their prosperity.

They don't have the pressures I have,

They have strong healthy bodies.

They don't let ethics bother them,

Nor do they have everyday problems.

They show off their selfish pride,

They will not stop at violence to get their way.

They lust for everything,

There is no satisfying their evil desires.

They scoff at everyone else,

They willingly use violence to get their way.

They claim to be bigger than Heaven,

They think everything on earth belongs to them.

They have deceived people

To believe everything they say.

They say, "God doesn't know everything,
   The Most High doesn't know what I do."
Lord, these are arrogant people
   Who have a life of ease, because of their money.

But, Lord, was I wrong to stay pure;
   When I denied myself the pleasures of evil?
I have had trouble all day long,
   Every morning I face a different trial.
If I have the attitude of the wicked,
   I would have betrayed Your children.
I try to figure out why the wicked prosper,
   But I only become more confused.

Then I come into Your presence in the sanctuary,
   And I understand their future destiny.
Now I realize they are on a slippery path,
   They are heading toward eternal destruction.
They will die and instantly be punished,
   And will be consumed by terror.
One day, Lord, You will arise,
   To punish their selfish desires.

Lord, I acknowledge how bitter I had become,
   My whole outlook was poisoned by hatred.
I was reacting like a dumb animal,
   I didn't know what I was doing.
Nevertheless, I still follow You;
   You have always held me with Your right hand.
You have guided me with Your counsel,
   And one day You will receive me into glory.

I don't have anyone in Heaven but You,

    I desire nothing on earth but You.

My flesh will get weak and my heart will fail,

    But You are the strength of my life.

Those who will not follow You will perish,

    Because You will destroy those who reject You.

But it is good for me to be near You,

    I have made You my shelter;

    I will tell everyone of Your works.

                      Amen

*A Psalm of Asaph.

PSALM 74

*A Prayer To Recognize The Power Of God And Call On Him To Crush Your Enemies**

Lord, why have You rejected us?

    Why are You angry against the sheep of Your pasture?

Remember, we are the people You redeemed;

    You chose to give us an inheritance,

    You came to dwell in Mt. Zion.

Now, walk through the destruction of Jerusalem;

    See how the enemy has destroyed Your sanctuary.

Your enemies claimed victory in the place You met with us,

    They took over the place where You once dwelt.

They cut down Your holy place with axes,

    Like it was a grove of trees.

They smashed the beautiful carved fixtures,

    With their axes and battle hammers.

They burned Your sanctuary with fire,

Then defiled the place where Your name dwells.
They said inwardly, "Let's completely destroy this place";
     They have destroyed every other place You are
     worshipped in the land.

Lord, where are Your miracles;
     Don't You have any prophets left?
     We don't know what to do.
Lord, how long will the enemy mock You;
     Will You allow them to embarrass You forever?
Why are You holding back Your hand of judgment?
     Why don't You destroy them?

You, O God, have always been king;
     You bring salvation to the earth.
You divided the Red Sea by Your power,
     You smash the sea creatures' heads.
You crushed the heads of the Leviathan
     And let the other animals eat him.
You gave Your people water from the rock,
     You held back the mighty Jordan River.
The day is Yours, as well as the night;
     You created light and gave us the sun.
You established the boundaries of the earth,
     You make both summer and winter.

Look at how Your enemy mocks You,
     These foolish people blaspheme Your name.
Do not let innocent doves be devoured by beasts,
     Don't let Your persecuted people be eaten alive.
Remember the covenant You made with Your people,
     Because dark times and violence threaten us.

Don't let us retreat in shame,

    The poor and needy want to praise Your name.

O God, get up to defend Your cause;

    Because these fools are mocking You.

You can't ignore the threats of Your enemies,

    Their defiance is getting louder and louder.

Amen

*A Psalm of instruction by Asaph.

PSALM 75

*A Prayer That Recognizes God's Punishment Of The Wicked And His Protection Of The Humble**

I give You thanks, O God;

    I am thankful that You are near

    To tell about Your wonderful works.

You will receive the people,

    You will judge the people correctly.

When the earthquakes destroy all human order,

    You will hold everything together. Selah!

You warned the arrogant to stop boasting,

    You told the wicked to stop sinning.

You told the proud to be humble,

    And not stiffen their neck toward You.

Because exaltation doesn't come from the east or west,

    Nor does it come from the south;

But it is You that knows the heart,

    You bring one person down, but exalt another.

In Your hand is a cup of judgment,

It is seething with punishment.

You pour it out on everyone,

But the wicked must drink the last terrible dregs.

As for me, I will tell everyone what You have done;

I will sing praises to You, O God.

You will cut off the boasting of the wicked,

But the godly will be exalted.

Amen

*A Psalm or song of Asaph.

PSALM 76

*A Prayer Of Praise To God Because He Judges Rebellion**

God, Your name is known across Judah;

Your name is greatly respected throughout Israel.

Your tent is pitched in peace,

You live in Mount Zion.

There You stopped the attacks against us,

We no longer needed our defense. Selah!

You are more glorious than light,

You are more excellent than the mountains.

The strong warriors have been killed,

They sleep their final sleep;

Not one can lift his hand in war.

At Your rebuke, O God of Jacob;

All the dangers of war are stilled.

You are the only One to be feared,
  No one can stand before Your anger.
You announced the verdict from Heaven,
  The land heard it quietly in awe;

Because You arose in judgment
  To save all those who trusted You. Selah!
Then You will be praised because of men's rebellious anger,
  Because Your greater anger against them will be unrestrained.

I will fulfill the vows I make to You, O Lord God;
  Accept the gifts that we all bring to You.
I know You will crush the rebellion of rulers,
  They will all fear Your terrible judgment.

Amen

*A Psalm or song of Asaph.

PSALM 77

*A Prayer For Deliverance**

I cried to You for help, O God;
  I begged for You to listen to my prayers.
I sought You, O Lord, in my day of trouble,
  I couldn't sleep at night;
  And I couldn't be comforted.

When I remembered what You could do,
  My spirit was overwhelmed with agony. Selah!
I couldn't sleep at night because of my trouble,
  I was too concerned to pray.

I thought back to the way You did things,
How You always helped Your people.
I remembered when I sang in the night,
How I meditated on Your presence.

Why have You cast me away?
Will You ever come back to me again?
Is Your mercy completely exhausted?
Will You keep Your promise again?
Have You forgotten how to be gracious?
Has Your anger shut up Your mercy? Selah!

Then I concluded that I was getting what I deserved,
But I will remember the years Your right hand helped me.
I will meditate on all Your works,
I will remember all the miracles You did in the past.

You still live in Your sanctuary, O God;
No man-made god is as great as You.
You are the God who does miracles,
You have shown Your strength among Your people,
You have redeemed Your people, the sons of
Jacob and Joseph. Selah!

The Red Sea trembled before You, O God;
It was ready to obey Your command.
The rain clouds poured on our enemies,
The thunder roared and the lightning flashed.
Your judgment was heard in the whirlwind,
You lit up the night with lightning;
The ground shook with an earthquake.

You led Your people through the Red Sea,

    Although no one saw Your footprints.

You led Your people like a flock,

    You led by the hand of Moses and Aaron.

Amen

*A Psalm of Asaph.

PSALM 78

*A Prayer That Recognizes God's Faithfulness In The Face Of Israel's Unfaithfulness**

Lord, I want the people to listen to Your teaching

    So they can hear what You're saying;

For You speak to them in parables,

    You communicate by hidden ways from the past.

What we have heard and known,

    The lessons our fathers have told me.

We will not hide them from our children,

    We will tell the generations to come

    About the praises due to You, O Lord.

    Because of the glorious deeds You have done,

You establish the testimony of Jacob

    And You decreed the law for Israel.

Then You commanded our forefathers

    To teach it to their children.

So the coming generations would know the law,

    Even their children not yet born;

So they in turn would tell their children,

    With a result that they would trust You, O God.

That coming generations would not forget Your works,

But keep the commandments You have given;
So they would not be like their forefathers,
　Who were a stubborn and rebellious generation
Who refused to yield their hearts to You;
　Whose spirits did not want to obey You.

The men of Ephraim had superior armament,
　But retreated in the day of battle.
They did not keep their covenant with You,
　And refused to walk in Your law.
They forgot what You had done for them.
　And the miracles by which You delivered them
You did marvelous things in the presence of their fathers,
　In the land of Egypt and in the land of Zoan.
You divided the Red Sea for them to escape,
　You held the waters back like a wall.
You guided them with a cloud by day,
　And a pillar of fire at night.
You split the rock in the desert,
　To give them abundant water.
You brought a stream of water out of the rock,
　Causing water to run down like a river.

But our forefathers sinned against You,
　Rebelling in the wilderness against You, the Most High God.
The obstinate tested You,
　Demanding meat to satisfy their lust.
They ask in unbelief,
　"Can God spread a table in the wilderness?"
When Moses struck the rock,
　A stream of water gushed out.
But they in unbelief doubted if You could feed them,

Doubting if You could supply food.
You were very angry when You heard them,
    A consuming fire broke out against them;
For they did not believe You could provide for them,
    Nor did they trust You to deliver them.
You commanded the skies to open,
    And you rained down manna for them to eat;
    It was the corn of Heaven.
They ate the food of angels,
    They had all the food they wanted.
You sent a strong East wind,
    Then You directed a mighty wind from the South.
You blew food on them like a sandstorm,
    Flying birds were like sand on a seashore.
The birds flew in low through their tents,
    They landed all around their tents.
Our forefathers ate until they were filled,
    You gave them all they desired.
But even when the food You supplied was in their mouth,
    They were lusting for more.
Your wrath was unleashed against them,
    You put to death the strongest and best.

And they still kept on sinning,
    In spite of Your miracles, they wouldn't trust You.
So they died needlessly in the wilderness,
    They lived in constant terror.
Whenever You judged some of them,
    Those who were left would eagerly turn to You.
They remembered that You were their Rock,
    That the Most High God was their Redeemer.
They flattered You with their lips,

But they were lying in their hearts.
Because their hearts were rebellious toward You,
    They did not intend to keep their covenant with You.
Yet You were merciful toward them,
    You held back Your anger.
You remembered that they were just human,
    They're just a breeze that's quickly gone.

They often provoked You in the desert,
    They grieved You during the forty years in the wilderness.
They constantly rebelled against You,
    Continually frustrating You, the Holy One of Israel.
They forgot what You did for them.
    They didn't remember how You delivered them
    By the mighty miracles in Egypt,
    Or the wonders against pharaoh in Zoan.
You turned Egypt's streams into blood,
    No one could drink from them.
You sent swarms of flies among them,
    And frogs that frustrated them.
You sent grasshoppers to eat their crops,
    And locusts devoured all they grew.
You sent sleet to destroy their vines,
    And hail to ruin the sycamore figs.
Also, their cattle died in the hail,
    And lightning killed their livestock.
You released Your anger against them,
    Sending a band of destroying angels among them.
You made a way to express Your anger,
    You did not spare them from death.
You killed the firstborn in every family,
    The oldest male child of every Egyptian family died.

Then You led Your own people out of Egypt,
Guiding them safely into the desert.
Your people were safe as You led them,
But their enemies were drowned in the Red Sea.
You brought them to the border of the promised land,
You gave them the hill country as their own.
You drove out the heathen before them
And divided the land to them as an inheritance,
You settled each tribe into its home.

But they refused to obey You, the Most High God;
They refused to keep Your commandments.
Like their fathers, they were faithless and rebellious,
They were as unreliable as a faulty weapon.
They made high places to worship other gods,
They angered You with their man-made idols.
When You saw this, You were again angry;
You completely rejected them.
You withdrew from the Tabernacle in Shiloh
The tent where You had met with Your people.
You allowed the enemy to defeat Your people,
Because You were angry with Your inheritance.
The fire consumed the young men,
And the young women did not marry.
The priests were killed by the sword,
And the widows did not grieve for them.

Then You awoke, as it was from Your sleep;
As a man awakens from a deep sleep.
You routed the enemies and they retreated,
You put them away forever.
You didn't bring the Deliverer from the tent of Joseph,

Nor did You choose the tent of Ephraim;
But You chose the tribe of Judah.

You chose Mount Zion to be Your home.

You put Your sanctuary there among the high places,
You chose that place among all the places on earth.

You chose David to be Your leader,
You brought him from leading sheep
To be the shepherd of Your people.

And David will lead Israel with the integrity of his heart,
And guide them by the skillfulness of his hands.

Amen

*A Psalm of instruction by Asaph.

PSALM 79

A Prayer For God To Punish
*Those Who Persecute Israel**

O God, the heathen nations have conquered Your inheritance;
They have defiled Your holy temple,
They have made Jerusalem a trash heap.

They have left the dead bodies of Your followers
For the birds to eat,
The scavenger animals are eating them.

Their blood flowed around Jerusalem
And there was none to bury them.

Our neighbors are making fun of us,
Your people are being scorned.

Lord, how long will You be angry with Your people?
Will Your jealousy burn forever?

Pour out Your wrath on the nations that reject You,

And upon the people that refuse to call upon You.

For they have devoured Israel,

   And destroyed Your homeland.

Do not hold the sins of our father against us,

   Come quickly to deliver us;

   Because we need Your help now.

Help us, O God our Savior;

   And bring glory to Your name.

Forgive us our sins and deliver us

   For the sake of Your name.

Why should the heathen nations boast,

   "Where is their God?"

Pour out Your vengeance on them,

   Because they poured out the blood of Your servants.

Listen to the groans of the prisoners,

   Save them before they die.

Retaliate against our enemies seven times,

   Giving them the misery they have caused us.

We are Your people, the sheep of Your pasture;

   We will thank and praise You forever.

Amen

*A Psalm of Asaph.

PSALM 80

A Prayer For God To Deliver
*The Rebellious People Of Israel**

Listen to us, O Shepherd of Israel;

   You lead the sons of Joseph like a flock;

You are enthroned between the cherubim,

    Shine forth.

Stir up Your strength before Ephraim, Benjamin, and Manasseh,

    Come and save us.

Turn us around, O God;

    Shine Your face upon us to save us.

O Lord God of the angels,

    How long will You be angry against our prayers?

We are eating the bread of anguish,

    And we are drinking tears.

We are trouble to our neighbors,

    Our enemies laugh at us.

Turn us around, O God of angels;

    Shine Your face upon us to save us.

We were the cutting of a vine,

    You brought us out of Egypt.

You drove the heathen out of the promised land,

    Then planted us there.

You cleared the ground so we could grow,

    We took root and thrived.

The mountains were covered by our cool shade,

    Our branches reached out like gigantic trees.

We reached out to the seas,

    Then we extended our rule to the rivers.

Why did You take away our protective wall

    So strangers could pick our fruit?

Pigs are rooting up our vine,

    Wild animals are eating up our leaves.

Come back to us, O God of the angels;
    Look down from Heaven on us,
    Come protect this vine.
Come back to the vineyard You planted,
    Send the Son who is Your Deliverer.

You have trimmed the vine and thrown it into the fire,
    Your people are dying under Your punishment.
Send the man who sits on Your right hand,
    The son of man who is strong to deliver.
Then we will not turn away from You,
    Restore us so we can call upon Your name.
Turn us around, O Lord God of the angels;
    Shine Your face upon us to save us.

                     Amen

*A Psalm of Asaph.

PSALM 81

A Prayer Of Grateful Worship
*Because You Realize Your Past Rebellion**

I sing loudly to You, O God my strength;
    I shout praises to You, O God of Jacob.
I sing a hymn and play the tambourine,
    I play praise choruses to You on the guitar.
I blow the trumpet in celebration,
    And I confess my sin in the solemn assembly.
This is the right way for me to worship,
    This is the way I fulfill Your law, O God.

You directed Israel to worship this way,
    When You brought us out of Egypt;

Where we heard a language we didn't understand.
You took the burden from our shoulder,
   You freed us from their flesh pots.
We called out to You in our distress,
   And You answered us from the dark cloud.

Then You tested us at the waters of Meribah, Selah!
   You called out to warn us,
   You wanted us to listen to You.
You commanded us not to possess foreign idols,
   Nor should we worship any strange gods.
You are the Lord our God
   Who brought us up out of Egypt.

You promised to fill our lives,
   If we would just open ourselves up to You.
But we would not listen to Your voice,
   And we would not yield to Your leadership.
So You gave us over to our sinful hearts,
   You let us make our own decisions.

If we would have just listened to You,
   And obeyed Your principles.
You would have defeated our enemies,
   And strengthened our hand against our foes.
Those who hate You would have feared You,
   Because You would have punished them.
You would have fed us with the best food,
   And satisfied us with honey from the Rock.

                                             Amen

*A Psalm of Asaph.

PSALM 82

*A Plea For God To Set All Things Right**

O God, You stand in Heaven's courtroom;
   You can correctly evaluate the gods.
How long will You withhold judgment
   And let the wicked continue living? Selah!
Defend the poor and the fatherless,
   Protect the afflicted and needy.
Deliver them in their time of affliction,
   And from the clutches of the wicked.
They don't know what's happening,
   They walk blindly in darkness;
   Because the foundation of the earth is out of whack.
I told them, "You all belong to God;
   You are all the children of the Most High."
Because they will not listen, they will die as all others,
   And be buried as are the powerful rulers.
Come, O God, judge all people;
   Because all people are Your inheritance.

Amen

*A Psalm of Asaph.

PSALM 83

A Prayer For God To Destroy
His Enemies And Rule The Earth

O God, do not keep quiet and still;
   Why are You so silent?
Your enemies are causing trouble,
   They that hate You are threatening us.

They have conspired against us,

They devise evil against Your chosen ones.

They boast that they can destroy us,

That the nation of Israel will not be remembered.

They all plan together against You,

They join together to destroy Your influence.

The people of Edom, Ishmael, Moab, and the Hagites,

Join with Gebal, Ammon, Amalek, and Philistia.

They have joined together with Tyre and Assyria,

To strengthen the sons of Lot. Selah!

Defeat them as You did the Midianites,

As You defeated Sisera and Jabin at Kisham.

May they die today as they died at Endor,

They became as fertilizer on the ground.

Make their leaders like Oreb and Zeeb,

As You destroyed Zebah and Zalmunna.

They boasted they would capture

Your Sanctuary as their possessions.

O God, make Your enemies like weeds;

As chaff which the wind blows away.

Consume them like fire burns wood,

Like the forest fires consume the mountains.

So punish them with Your terror,

Beat upon them with Your storm.

Humiliate all their endeavors,

So that they will seek Your name, O Lord.

Confuse everything they do,

So that they will forever be tormented.

Make them realize that Your name is Jehovah,

That You alone rule as the Most High over the earth.

Amen

HOW TO PRAY

When You Want To Be Happy: Psalm 84:4

There are two words for *blessed* in the original language of the Psalms. First, *barak,* is the usual word used for blessed and comes from "to bow," as subjects bowing before a King because they want something from the King. They know the King can bless their lives. This word means to be enriched, or to receive value, or to have your life filled or fulfilled. As you pray the Psalms, bow before God, asking Him to fill your life with the things for which the Psalmist originally prayed. *Lord, bless me indeed.*

The second word for bless is *ashrey,* which means happiness. When God blesses you with ashrey you are positive, upbeat, i.e., you just feel good. *Lord, I want to feel good. Teach me what I must do to be happy.*

Because we all sin and disobedience is hard, and because life has many troubles, it's difficult to be happy all the time. But when we begin to trust the Lord, we begin to learn inner joy, "Happy [*ashrey*] is he who has the God of Jacob for his help, whose hope is in the Lord his God" (Ps. 146:5). *Lord, I trust You for today.*

Blessed is the man that walketh not in the counsel of the ungodly, nor standeth in the way of sinners, nor sitteth in the seat of the scornful (Ps. 1:1 KJV).

The very first word in the Book of Psalms is "happy", *ashrey.* This book will make you happy when you pray its words and follow its directions. Therefore, to be happy, there are three progressive actions you shouldn't do: (1) Walk not . . . (2) Stand not . . . and (3) Sit not. *Lord, I will get close to You, and stay away from sin.* There are three progressive attachments with ungodly people you should avoid: (1) Listen to their counsel . . . (2) Linger in their way . . . and (3) Settle down in their seat. *Lord, don't let me get attached to wicked people.* There are three progressively evil types of people to avoid: (1) Ungodly ... (2) Sinners ... and (3) Scorners. *Lord, show me the types of people I'm around, help me to understand their desire in life, and help me to separate from those who influence me to evil.*

You will be happy when you properly deal with your sin by confessing and turning from it. "Blessed [happy, *ashrey*] is he whose transgression is forgiven, whose sin is covered" (Ps. 32:1). *Lord, I confess my sin; please forgive me.*

You will be happy when you study the Scriptures and seek God's presence in prayer. "Oh, taste and see that the Lord is good; blessed [happy, *ashrey*] is the man who trusts in Him!" (Ps. 34:8) *Lord, I turn from my misery to You. I come to You with arms wide open. Hug me.*

You will be happy when you obey your inner urge to do God's will, because the Lord put that inner urge in you. "Blessed [happy, *ashrey*] is the man You choose, and cause to approach You, that he may dwell in Your courts. We shall be satisfied with the goodness of Your house, of Your holy temple" (Ps. 65:4). *Lord, I say "yes" to the inclination of my heart to worship You. I am very happy in Your presence. Thank You for pulling me to Yourself.*

The Psalmist describes a sparrow making a nest in the sanctuary, near the presence of God. The Temple was so peaceable, the sparrow made a nest, laying eggs, and going about her normal duties. The Psalmist wanted to be as close to God in the Temple, as was the sparrow. The Psalmist described the intimacy he wanted with God on a continuous basis. "My soul longs, yes, even faints for the courts of the Lord ... even the sparrow has found a home, and the swallow a nest for herself, where she may lay her young—even Your altars, O Lord of hosts, my King and my God" (Ps. 84:2-3). The Psalmist is crying out to enjoy the peace he finds in God's presence. *Lord, I love Your presence.*

You will be happy like the Psalmist when you stay in God's presence to enjoy intimacy with Him. "Blessed are those who dwell in Your house; they will still be praising You" (Ps. 84:4). *Lord, I am comfortable in Your presence.*

The world's happiness is only a feeling that gets you excited and makes you temporarily forget your problems. But after the world's happiness is over, the troubles of life return because, "Man who is born of woman is of few days and full of trouble" (Job 14:1). But the happiness that God gives is lasting, because God is the giver and He goes with you. "Blessed [happy, *ashrey*] is the man whose strength is in You" (Ps. 84:5). *Lord, I am happy at this moment because I am in Your presence. Lord, go with me to keep me happy along life's way.*

"Happy are the people who are in such a state [who obey the Lord]; happy are the people whose God is the Lord" (Ps. 144:15).

(For your study look up the word *ashrey*, i.e., happy, in the following verses; Ps. 1:1; 2:12; 32:1-2; 33:12; 34:8; 40:4; 41:1; 65:4; 84:4-5, 12; 89:15; 94:12; 106:3; 112:1; 119:1-2; 127:5; 128:1-2; 137:8-9; 144:15; 146:5.)

PSALM 84

*A Prayer To Enjoy God's Presence In His House**

Lord, I enjoy coming into Your presence in the Tabernacle;
> O Lord of hosts.

I have such a deep passion for the courts of Your presence
> That my flesh cries out when I'm not there.

Lord, the sparrows are so comfortable in Your presence;
> That they make their nest within sight of Your altar.

I also want to rest near Your presence,
> Because You are my King and my God.

Lord, bless those who stay in Your house;
> Because they worship and praise You. Selah!

Lord, bless those who realize their strength is in You;
> Because Your principles are in their heart.

Lord, they come to You through a valley of weeping;
> They fill pools with their tears.

Lord, they continue climbing from strength to strength
> In their endeavor to find Your peace.

Lord God, my desire is to know You;
> And to look into Your face. Selah!

For one day in the courts of Your presence,
> Is better than a thousand days anywhere else.

I would rather be a doorkeeper in Your house,
> Than live sumptuously in the tents of wickedness.

Lord, You shine warmth on my life like the sun;

>   You protect me like a shield.

You will not withhold any good thing from me,

>   If I walk uprightly.

Blessed are those who trust in You.

>   Amen

*A Psalm for the sons of Korah.

PSALM 85

*A Prayer For God To Forgive Our Sins And Bring Peace To The Earth**

O Lord, You have shown favor to Your land;

>   You brought back Jacob from captivity.

You forgave the iniquity of Your people,

>   And covered all their sins. Selah!

You are no longer angry at us,

>   You have turned aside Your wrath.

Turn us to You, O God our Savior;

>   And stop punishing us.

Will You be angry with us forever?

>   Will You always continue punishing us?

Revive our spirits, O God;

>   That we may rejoice in You.

Show us Your mercy, O Lord;

>   And save us from our troubles.

I will listen to what You say,

>   To Your promises of peace for Your people;

>   Lord, don't let us return to folly.

You will surely save those who fear You,

So Your glory can live in the land.
Then mercy and truth will meet each other,
Righteousness and peace will kiss.
Truth will be found in the earth,
And righteousness will look down from Heaven.
You will give us what is good, O Lord;
And we will prosper in this land.
Righteousness will go before You,
To prepare all the ways that You go.

Amen

*A Psalm for the sons of Korah.

PSALM 86

*A Prayer For Help In The Face Of Danger**

O Lord, bend down low to hear me;
For I am poor and needy.
Protect my soul, for I am separated from You;
Save me because I am Your servant.
O God, have mercy on me;
For I pray to You all the time.
Give me joy, O Lord;
For I lift my soul to You.

You are a forgiving and good Lord,
You give mercy to all who call on You.
Listen to my prayer, O Lord;
And hear what I am saying to You.
In my day of trouble I call on You,
Because You will answer and do something for me.

There is none like You among the earthly gods,

    They cannot do the works that You do.

You have made all the different ethnic groups of people,

    They will come before You to worship

    And bring glory to Your name.

For You are great and do awesome works,

    You alone are God.

O Lord, teach me the way I should walk;

    And I will follow Your truth.

Give me a focused heart,

    So I will fear Your name.

I will praise You with my whole heart, O Lord my God;

    I will glorify Your name forever.

For Your mercy is great to me,

    You have delivered me from the lowest hell.

The boastful are coming to attack me,

    They are violent men who want to destroy me;

    They do not honor You

But You, Lord, are a compassionate God;

    You are patient with abundant love and kindness.

Come to me in mercy and give me strength,

    Save the son of Your handmaid.

Show me a sign that You are with me,

    Confuse my enemies, then help and comfort me, O Lord.

                                Amen

*A prayer of David.

PSALM 87

A Prayer Of Thanksgiving
*For Being Born In God's City**

You established a firm foundation on Your holy mountain,
    You love the gates of Zion
More than all the houses of Judah, O God;
    Glorious things are spoken of Your city.
    Zion is Your city, O God. Selah!
Those from Rahab and Babylon take notice,
    Along with those from Philistia, Tyre, and Cush;
    That I was born in Jerusalem.
Even in Zion they will recognize
    That I was born in Jerusalem.
Jerusalem is the city of the Most High,
    He will establish it forever.
Even You, Lord, register those people
    Who were born in Zion. Selah!
The singers and musicians praise You, O Lord;
    All my life is dedicated to You.

                                        Amen

*A Psalm or song for the sons of Korah.

PSALM 88

A Prayer Of Confession And Anguish
*From One Being Punished By God**

I have cried out to You day and night,
    Save me, O Lord God.
Receive my prayer into Your presence,

Listen to the request I am making.
I have all kinds of troubles,
    They are continually trying to kill me.
People treat me like I'm already dead,
    Like I have no strength left.
They abandoned me like a corpse,
    Like someone who is not here
    And gone out of their sight forever.

Have You put me into this hole,
    Into this dark night?
I feel Your anger punishing me,
    Coming one wave of pain after another. Selah!
You have taken away my friends,
    Now they all hate me;
    I'm in a hole and can't get out.
I am blinded by my tears,
    Each day I call out to You;
    I lift my hands pleading for help.

Will You show the miracles You do for the dead
    Because the dead can rise again to praise You? Selah!
Shall Your kindness extend to those in a hole
    Because You are faithful even in punishment?
Can You show Your wonders to those in dark places
    Because You never forget those who are forgotten?

I cried to You for help, O Lord;
    Every morning I pray again to You.
Why do You not hear me,
    And hide Your face from me?
I hurt all over and am ready to die,

I can't stand Your punishment any longer.

Your fierce anger has overwhelmed me,

 I am cut to the bone.

All day long my sin haunts my memory,

 I am completely overwhelmed with fear.

You have taken away my friends and relatives,

 And darkness is my only companion.

Amen

*A Psalm of instruction by Heman the Ezrahite.

PSALM 89

*A Prayer For God To Remember The Promise He Made To David**

Lord, I will continually sing of Your mercies;

 I will make known Your faithfulness forever,

 All generations will hear it from my mouth.

I will testify that Your mercy stands forever,

 That Your faithfulness is as firm as Heaven itself.

You made a covenant with Your chosen One,

 You swore an oath with David Your servant.

You promised to establish his family lineage forever,

 You promised to give the throne of Israel to him. Selah!

The heavens praise You, O Lord;

 Your faithfulness is revealed where angels gather.

No one in the heavens compares with You, O Lord;

 None of the mighty angels is likened unto You.

You are greatly feared among the angelic beings,

 You are more awesome than all those about Your throne.

O Lord God of the angels, who is likened unto You?

   Your faithfulness is seen in all You do.

You rule the raging sea,

   When the storms blow, you still them.

You destroy the great sea monsters,

   You scatter Your enemies with a strong arm.

The heavens are Yours, so is the earth;

   You established the universe and everything in it.

You made the north where it is, and the south;

   Mount Tabor and Hermon praise Your name.

You have a powerful arm and a mighty hand,

   You lift Your right hand in victory.

Your rule is characterized by righteousness and justice,

   Mercy and truth come from You.

Lord, bless those who sing joyfully to You;

   Who walk in the light of Your countenance.

They rejoice in Your name all day long,

   Therefore, You accept them.

You are their glory and strength,

   And You exalt them with Your anointing.

For You defend us from the evil one,

   You are our King, the Holy One of Israel.

You spoke in a vision to Your people,

   Telling them Your strength was upon a warrior;

   You lifted up a young man from among Your people.

You chose David as Your servant,

   You anointed him with oil to follow You.

You promised to strengthen him with Your hand,

   You established him with Your arm.

No enemy will make him pay tribute,

No wicked one will defeat him.
You will destroy his enemies before him,
    And punish those who hate him.
You will faithfully be with him,
    And Your name will be exalted by him.
You will give him the rule of the sea,
    And his right hand over the rivers.
David will call out to You as his God,
    Calling You his Father and the rock of his salvation.
You will appoint him as your firstborn,
    Higher than any king on earth.
You will maintain Your love to him forever,
    You will always keep the covenant You made with him.
You have established his genealogy forever,
    His throne will endure as long as Heaven exists.

If the children of David forsake Your law,
    And do not obey Your commandments;
If they violate Your directions,
    And do not keep Your rules;
Then You will punish their disobedience,
    And You will correct their rebellious ways.
But You will never stop loving them,
    Nor will You turn Your back on them.
You will not deny the promise You made to them,
    You will always keep Your Word.
You only had to give Your Word once,
    You will not lie to David.
You will bless his line forever,
    He will always rule for You.
It will be established forever like the sun and moon,
    Your faithful witnesses in the sky. Selah!

But You had to reject the covenant You made,

   Why did You get angry with Your people?

You turned Your back on Your covenant,

   You threw the crown of David to the ground.

You had to break down all their defenses,

   You have destroyed all their strongholds.

The passing armies have plundered Israel,

   Their neighbors laugh at Israel's weaknesses.

You strengthened Israel's enemies against her,

   You have let them become triumphant in battle.

You watched as Israel was weakened,

   Then You saw Your people defeated in battle.

You let Israel's glory fade,

   And You let her enemies terminate the rule of David's kingdom.

You cut short the days of his line,

   You gave him a robe of shame. Selah!

How long will You let Your people suffer?

   Will You continue to hide from us?

   Will Your anger burn forever?

Remember how short is our life,

   For You have created us with many limitations.

None of us can live and not die,

   None of us can overcome the power of death. Selah!

O Lord, where is Your former patient love

   That You pledged to David Your servant?

Look now, Lord, on the abuse we receive;

   We carry the insults of all Your enemies.

They mock us because they hate You,

They reject the rule of David Your anointed;

We bless You forever,

Amen and Amen.

*A Psalm of instruction by Ethan the Ezrahite.

PSALM 90

*A Prayer To Use The Time Allotted To You**

Lord, You have been our dwelling place;

Throughout all the generations.

Before You created the mountains,

Even before You created the earth,

Even from everlasting to everlasting;

You are God.

You determined that all people will die,

You decreed that we would all return to dust.

A thousand years in Your sight,

Is but yesterday that is gone;

It's just a watch in the night.

You carry away our years like a flood,

Our life is like sleep after we awake.

Our life is like grass that springs up in the morning,

We grow throughout the day;

In the evening we are cut down,

Then we wither and die.

Your anger can consume us,

Your wrath brings us trouble.

You see all of our disobediences,

You shine Your light on our secret sins.

When You are angry with us,

    Our life passes away quickly.

Our simple life does not amount to much,

    Like a tale that someone tells.

We live approximately three score and ten years,

    Some reach the golden age of four score years.

But they have physical difficulties and pain,

    Then their life is cut off and they fly away.

No one knows when You are angry at them,

    So we must always trust You in fear.

So teach us to make each day count,

    So that we can live wisely.

Return to bless us,

    Don't be angry with us any longer.

Show us mercy when we are young,

    So we may rejoice all our lives.

May we learn from the years You afflicted us,

    And from the years we sinned against You.

Help us understand Your works,

    Show Your glory to our children.

O Lord God, let Your beauty be upon us;

    Establish the work of our hands,

    Yes, the work of our hands establish Thou.

                      Amen

*A prayer of Moses the man of God.

PSALM 91

A Prayer For Protection From Constant Danger Of Daily Life

When I live in the secret place of Your presence,

O Most High God who owns the universe;

I abide under Your protective shadows,

O Almighty God who is more than enough.

Lord, I will testify about the results of Your presence,

You are my protection and fortress;

You are my God in whom I trust.

I know You will save me from all traps,

And from deadly diseases.

You will cover me with Your wings,

I will find refuge under Your protection;

Your promises give me peace and security.

I will not be afraid of the unseen terror by night,

Nor of the ever present dangers of the day.

Nor of the lurking plagues that threaten me,

Nor of the spreading epidemic around me.

A thousand may fall at my side,

And ten thousand may die around me;

But these dangers will not come near me.

I will observe with my eyes,

And will see the punishment of the wicked.

I will make You, O Most High God,

My protective refuge.

And when You are my refuge, O Lord,

Then no harm can destroy me;

And the epidemic plague will not touch me.

Because You will command Your angels
   To guard me in all ways,
They will protect me with their hands,
   To keep me from falling.
I can trample down lions and poisonous snakes,
   I will crush evil threats under my feet.

Because I love You, Lord,
   You will rescue me from danger.
Because I know You by name,
   You will be with me in trouble.
When I call upon You for help,
   You will answer me.
   You will be with me.
   You will protect me and my honor.
You will give me long life,
   And satisfy me with Your salvation.

                              Amen

PSALM 92

*Praise To God For Giving You Strength**

Lord, it is good to praise You;
   To sing to Your name, O Most High.
To show Your loving kindness in the morning,
   And Your faithfulness in the evening.
To praise You with stringed instruments,
   By playing music upon the harp.
Lord, I rejoice in the things You do;
   I sing for joy because of what You have done.

O Lord, how great are Your works;

    Your thoughts are very deep.

The ignorant people do not know You,

    The foolish ones cannot understand You.

Even though they grow like weeds,

    And those that rebel against You flourish;

They will be forever destroyed,

    But You, Lord, are exalted forever.

Surely, O Lord, Your enemies are targeted;

    Surely Your enemies will perish,

    Those who are passionate for evil will be scattered.

You have exalted my strength like an ox,

    You have anointed me with fresh oil.

Mine eyes have seen the defeat of Your enemies,

    Mine ears have heard their destruction.

The righteous will flourish like a palm tree,

    They will grow like the cedars of Lebanon.

They that are planted in Your house,

    Will flourish in Your courts, O Lord.

They will bear fruit in their old age,

    They will stay fruitful and green.

Their life will testify that You are just,

    You are our Rock;

    You are always good to Your people.

                           Amen

*A Psalm or song for the Sabbath day.

PSALM 93

*A Prayer That Recognizes God's Power
Is Greater Than Anything On This Planet*

O Lord, You reign over all the earth;
    You are robed in majesty,
    You are clothed in power.
You have established the world,
    And it cannot be moved;
    You establish Your throne from eternity.
The seas have roared, O Lord;
    It has lifted up its voice,
    Its pounding waves crash on the shore.
But You, Lord on high, are mightier,
    More powerful than the flood;
    More powerful than the waves of the sea.
Your laws cannot be broken,
    Your rule is holy;
    You will reign for endless days.

                              Amen

PSALM 94

A Prayer For Patience Until God Judges Your Oppressors

O Lord, God, I know You avenge;
    O God, come and avenge now.
Rise up, Thou Judge of the earth,
    Punish the proud as they deserve.

How long will the wicked get by, O Lord;
　　How long will they gloat over us?
Do You hear them boasting over us?
　　The evil workers brag about their evil.
They crush Your people, O Lord;
　　Stomping the life out of Your heirs.
They kill widows, foreigners, and orphans,
　　Saying the Lord does not see and
　　The God of Jacob doesn't care.

Lord, make the fools understand;
　　Make them understand what You will do.
You make the ear, can You not hear?
　　You created eyes, shall You not see?
You give us knowledge, do You not know?
　　You judge the nations, will You not punish them?
Lord, You know the thoughts of all people;
　　You know they have no reason for what they do.

O Lord, those You correct are blessed;
　　Because You teach them Your love.
You will give them peace in the day of trouble
　　Until the wicked dig a pit and fall into it.
You will not reject Your people,
　　Neither will You abandon Your heirs.
When judgment falls on Your righteous people,
　　Then the upright in heart will be revealed.

Who will testify for me against the evildoers,
　　Who will stand with me against the wicked?
Unless You help me, O Lord;
　　I would have no defense in judgment.

When I realized my foot was slipping,
    Your faithfulness helped me up.
When I was overwhelmed with anxiety,
    Your comfort gave me peace and joy.

Those ungodly oppressors claim You're on their side,
    But their rule is based on wickedness.
They attack those who live by Your laws,
    And kill innocent people who have not hurt them.
But You, Lord, are my defense,
    You are a mighty rock where I can hide.
You will punish them with the death they plan for others,
    You will destroy them for their sin;
    O Lord, my God, You will destroy them.

Amen

*Translated by the author just after the terrorist attack on the Twin Towers in New York City.

PSALM 95

A Prayer Of Praise To God And Warning To The Wicked

I come singing to You, Lord;
    I shout joyfully to You,
    The Rock of my salvation.
I come into Your presence giving thanks,
    I shout the Psalms joyfully to You.
For You are my great God,
    The great King above earthly gods.
You hold the deep places of the earth in Your hands,
    You own the tops of the hills.

You made the sea and it is Yours,
  And You created all dry ground.

I come bowing down to worship You,
  I kneel before You, my Creator.
For You are my God,
  And I am like Your sheep;
  I am like the people of Your pasture.
Today, those who hear Your voice
  Should not provoke You by hardening their hearts,
  As Israel did when tempted in the wilderness.
The leaders of Israel saw Your miracles,
  But gave into temptation during their wanderings.

For forty years You were grieved with that generation,
  Because they were rebellious in heart;
  They did not know Your ways.
You determined to judge them,
  Not allowing them to enter the promised land.

                                    Amen

PSALM 96

A Prayer To Recognize God Rules Everything And Every Person

I sing a new song to You, Lord,
  The whole earth is singing to You.
I sing to bless Your name,
  And tell Your salvation from day to day.
I declare Your glory to the unsaved,
  And tell them everything that You do.

For You, Lord, are great in the earth,
    You must be praised greatly;
    You must be feared more than other gods.

The gods of the unsaved are idols,
    But You created the heavens.
Honor and majesty belong to You,
    Strength and beauty are in Your sanctuary.
All people must give glory to You, Lord;
    All must give You glory and strength.
They must give You glory that is due to You,
    And bring sacrifice when they enter Your presence.

I worship You, Lord, in the beauty of Your holiness;
    All the unsaved should fear You.
I tell the unsaved that You reign,
    No one can move the earth that You established;
    You will correctly judge each person.
The heavens rejoice and the earth is glad,
    The sea waves roar at Your command.
The fields give forth Your goodness,
    The forest rejoices in Your care.

You are coming to judge all things,
    You will correctly judge the world;
    You will reward people according to truth.

                                   Amen

PSALM 97

A Prayer Of Rejoicing That Recognizes The Future Reign Of The Lord

O Lord, You reign; let the earth rejoice;
  Let the distant shores be glad.
You are surrounded by a cloud of thick darkness,
  Your throne is built on righteousness and justice.
Your attributes are a purifying fire,
  To consume everything that opposes You.

You reveal Yourself like flashes of lightning,
  So everyone can see Your holiness and tremble.
The mountains melt like wax before You,
  Because You are the Lord of the earth.
The heavens reveal Your righteousness,
  Everyone sees Your glory.
Those who worship idols will be ashamed,
  Those who glory in their idols
  Will recognize Your majestic glory.

Zion will hear and be glad,
  Also the cities of Judah will rejoice;
  Because You will judge correctly.
For You, Lord, are Most High over the earth;
  You are exalted over all the false gods.
Lord, may those who love You, hate evil;
  Guard those who are faithful to You,
  Deliver them from the evil one.
Shine Your light upon the godly,
  And Your blessings on those who do right.

Lord, may Your people rejoice in You;

And praise Your holy name.

Amen

PSALM 98

*A Prayer Of Worship To God From All Sources**

I sing a new song to You, Lord;

For You have done marvelous things.

Your right hand and Your holy arm

Have saved me.

You have made Your salvation known,

And shown it to the nations.

You have remembered Your mercy,

And faithfulness to Israel.

Everyone in all places of the earth

Knows about Your salvation.

Everyone joyfully shouts Your praise,

They break into worship music to praise You.

Everyone sings unto You with the harp,

Everyone offers praise unto You with singing.

Everyone shouts for joy to You,

Sound the trumpets and blow the horns.

Let the sea praise You with its roar,

Let the earth and everyone join together

With the rivers to applaud You,

As the hills join with them in Your praise.

For You are coming to judge the earth,

   You will make everything right;

   You will judge people fairly.

Amen

*A Psalm.

PSALM 99

*A Prayer Recognizing God's Rule,
And Your Response To Him*

Lord, let the nations tremble, You reign in Heaven;

You sit between the cherubim,

   Let the earth shake.

Lord, You are great in Zion;

   You are exalted over everyone.

Let everyone praise Your great and awesome name,

   For You are holy.

Mighty King, You love justice;

   You created fairness.

In Jacob You have established justice and righteousness,

   O God, I exalt You as my Lord;

   I worship at Your feet,

   For You are holy.

Moses and Aaron were Your priests,

   Samuel also interceded to You.

They called on Your name,

   You answered them.

You spoke to them from the shekinah glory cloud,

They followed Your principles;

They kept the laws You gave them.

O Lord, my God, You answered them;

And You forgave them when they confessed,

But You punished them when they rebelled.

O Lord, my God, I exalt You

And worship in Your holy mountain,

O Lord, my God, You are holy.

Amen

PSALM 100

*A Prayer Of Gratitude When Entering God's Presence**

Lord, I shout with joy to You;

Everyone from every nation joins me.

I worship as I enter Your presence with singing

Because You, Lord, are my God.

Lord, You made us and we belong to You;

We are Your people and the sheep of Your pasture.

Lord, I come into Your gates giving thanks;

I enter the courts with praise.

I bless Your holy name

By giving thanks for all You've done for me.

Lord, You are good, Your mercy is everlasting;

And Your truth endures forever.

Amen

*A Psalm of praise.

PSALM 101

A Prayer Asking God For Help
*Because You Live Blamelessly**

I will sing of Your love and justice,
    I will sing to You, O Lord.
I will try to live without sin,
    When will You come help me?

I will try to live blamelessly,
    With my family and friends.
I will not look on evil,
    Nor satisfy myself with it.

I will hate the evil deeds of others
    That can tempt and addict me.
I will have nothing to do
    With evil people who lie.

Those who secretly slander their friends,
    I will turn my back on them.
Those who are selfish and proud,
    I will have nothing to do with them.

Lord, You see all the faithful
    Who live for You.
Those who live blamelessly
    Honor You by their lifestyle.

Those who are deceitful
    Will not dwell with You,
Those who lie and rebel against You,
    Will not stand in Your presence.

Every morning You search all hearts,
    To determine those who love wickedness.
Then You separate every evil doer,
    From the blessing of Your presence.

                                        Amen

*A Psalm of David.

HOW TO PRAY

When You Are Lonely:
Psalm 102

You're not strange because you feel lonely and lost. Many people have felt "cut off" from other people, even when they live in a city of many people or work in a place with other workers. Loneliness is not about environment or about no one nearby. Loneliness is about your inner self. It's what you feel. The Psalmist felt the loneliness you feel, "I'm like a lonely owl that's lost in the desert. I can't sleep at night, I'm as lonely as a solitary sparrow" (Ps. 102:6-7, PTP). *Lord, the only thing I know for sure is that I am lonely.*

When you're lonely nothing much matters. You have no happiness, and nothing is worth doing. "My food tastes like dirt, and my tears drip into what I drink" (Ps. 102:9, PTP). *Lord, why is everything I do empty?*

When you're lonely cry out to God. "Hear me when I pray, O Lord, listen to my request for help. Do not hide Your face from me" (Ps. 102:1-2, PTP). *Lord, I'm here by myself; I need You now.*

Realize the only One who knows you is God and in return you can know God. "But You Lord, will live forever" (Ps. 102:12, PTP). And you will live forever with God. Therefore, God knows who you are and He knows where you are. God knows you are lonely and He has a plan for your life. "Your servants and all their children will live forever" (Ps. 102:28, PTP). *Lord, You know me and how miserable I feel. Come make Yourself real to me.*

You need to know God sees you and will guide you. "He looked down from the height of His sanctuary" (Ps. 102:19). *Look, here I am, look on me.*

When you're lonely you hurt all over, sometimes you even hurt in your body. What you need is relationship. God made us social creatures, and everyone needs someone else. If your relationship to God is healthy, then you can make a healthy relationship to another person. Look at Psalm 23. It's about a relationship, i.e., a relationship between the Shepherd and sheep, which is a reflection of your relationship to the Lord. "The Lord is my shepherd; I shall not want" (Ps. 23:1). Did you see that phrase "shall not want"? Lonely people want a relationship; they want a lot of things. They want fun ... meaning ... and happy times. Okay, it all starts with a relationship. *Lord, I'm a lost sheep. Protect me. I need You.*

Do you know the 23rd Psalm? Notice how the relationship develops between a sheep and shepherd, between you and the Lord. "He leadeth me ... He maketh me lie down ... He restoreth my soul ..." *Lord, come lead me.* Then notice what the Shepherd does for you. "Thou art with me ... Thou preparest a table before me ... Thou anointest my head ...." *Lord, I'm lonely. Come take away my loneliness.*

What's the best antidote for loneliness? God promises a future relationship. "I will dwell in the house of the Lord forever."

PSALM 102

*The Prayer For Deliverance Of A Downtrodden Person Because He Recognizes God's Eternal Plan**

Hear me when I pray, O Lord;
  Listen to my request for help.
Do not hide Your face from me,
  When I am in trouble.

Don't turn away from me,
  But quickly answer me.
My days disappear like smoke,
  My bones hurt all the time.

My spirit is dying like cut grass,
  And I've lost my appetite to eat anything.
I groan all the time,
  And I'm just skin and bones.

WHEN YOU ARE LONELY   193

I'm like a lonely owl
　　That's lost in the desert.
I can't sleep at night,
　　I'm as lonely as a solitary sparrow.

My enemies continually criticize me,
　　They curse me and destroy my reputation.
My food tastes like dirt,
　　And my tears drip into what I drink.

Because of Your anger and punishment,
　　You have cast me aside.
My days are gone like the night shadows,
　　I am withering away like grass.

But You, Lord, will live forever;
　　You will be known in every generation.
You will arise to have compassion on Jerusalem,
　　You will show favor on her;
　　When the appointed time comes.

You love every stone in Zion's walls,
　　You even love the dust of her streets.
The nations will tremble before Your name,
　　All the kings will fear Your glory.

For You will rebuild Zion,
　　You will appear in Your glory.
You will finally answer the prayers of the downtrodden,
　　You will no longer turn Your back to their cry.

Let this be written for future generations,
So that a nation not yet born will praise You.
Let them write that You will look down from Heaven,
To hear the groans of Your persecuted people;
To redeem and give them freedom.
Then Your name will be declared in Zion,
You will be praised in Jerusalem;
Because a multitude of peoples and kingdoms
Will come to worship You, O Lord.

You have cut me down in mid-life,
You have weakened my strength.
So I cry to You who lives forever,
Do not cut me off while I am still young.

In the beginning, You laid the foundations of the earth;
The heavens are the work of Your hands.
They will cease, but You will continue;
They will wear out like old clothes.

You will then change to new clothes,
And throw them away like rags.
You remain forever the same,
And Your years will never end.

Your servants and all their children
Will live eternally in Your presence.
And their children's children
Will be established before You.

Amen

*A prayer of the afflicted, when he is overwhelmed, and pours out his complaint before the Lord.

PSALM 103

*A Prayer To Bless The Lord For His Nature And Good Acts To You**

I bless You, Lord, from the bottom of my soul;
  With all that is within me,
  I bless Your holy name.
I bless You, Lord, from the bottom of my soul;
  And I don't forget any of Your benefits.

You, Lord, forgive my sins;
  You heal all my diseases.
You, Lord, redeem my life from death;
  You crown my life with Your love and mercy.
You, Lord, satisfy me with good things;
  My life is renewed like an eagle.

You, Lord, give righteousness and justice
  To all who are persecuted;
You, Lord, make known Your principles to Moses;
  You showed Your works to the people of Israel.
You, Lord, are merciful and gracious;
  Slow to anger and full of love.
You, Lord, will not continually accuse us;
  Nor will You stay angry forever.
You, Lord, will not punish us as we deserve;
  Nor reward us according to our sins.

For as the heavens are high above the earth,
  So great is Your love for us.

As far as the east is from the west,

    You have removed our sin from us that far.

As a father takes care of his children,

    So You love those who trust You.

You know what we are made of,

    You remember that we are only dust.

As for us, our days on earth are like grass;

    We grow like a flower in the field.

The wind blows around us and we are gone,

    As though we were never here.

But Your love is from everlasting to everlasting,

    Upon those who love You;

    And upon their children's children.

It extends to those who keep Your covenant,

    Who remember to obey Your principles.

You, Lord, made the heavens Your throne;

    You rule over everything.

All the angels bless You, Lord;

    Your mighty ones who listen to Your Word.

All the heavenly armies of angels bless You, Lord,

    Those who serve You and carry out Your will.

All Your creation bless You, Lord;

    Everything in Your kingdom

    Joins my soul in blessing You, Lord.

                        Amen

*A Psalm of David.

PSALM 104

A Prayer To Bless The Lord
Because Of The Greatness Of Creation

I bless You, Lord, from the bottom of my soul;
    Because You, Lord God, are great.
You are clothed with majesty and splendor,
    Dressed in the garment of light.
You stretched out the heavens like a curtain,
    The roof of Your home extends above the rain.
You make the clouds Your chariot,
    You walk on the wings of the wind.
The angels are Your messengers,
    The flashes of lightning are Your servants.

You placed the earth on its foundation,
    It can never be moved.
You covered it with deep water like a garment,
    That covered the tallest mountains.
At Your command the waters receded,
    You spoke by the thunder and they withdrew.
The mountains rose into sight again,
    And the valleys appeared;
    Returning to the places You intended.
You then set a boundary for the sea,
    It will never flood the earth again.

You pour water into the ravines from the springs,
    Water gushes down the valleys.
You give drink to the animals of the forest,
    The wild donkeys quench their thirst.

The birds make their nest by the streams,
 They sing in the branches.
You rain on the mountains from Your heavenly home,
 Causing fruit to grow on the earth.
You make grass to grow for the cattle,
 And vegetables to grow for us;
 Bringing food out of the earth.

You bring wine that gladdens our heart
 And oil to make our face shine,
 And bread to strengthen us.
Your trees are well watered,
 You cause the cedars of Lebanon to grow.
The birds make their nest in her branches,
 The stork makes its home in the pine trees.
The high mountains are for the goats,
 The rock badgers hide in the rocky cliffs.

You made the moon to tell us the seasons,
 And the sun follows a prescribed pattern.
When You bring the night, darkness follows;
 Then all the beasts of the forest prowl.
The hungry lion roars after its prey,
 It is You, O Lord, who controls all.
The wild animals hide when the sun rises,
 They retreat to their dens when it is light.
But men go out to work when the day comes,
 There he labors until the evening.

In Your wisdom You made them all, O Lord;
 The earth is full of Your creatures.
There is the wide and spacious sea,

In it are numerous creatures, small and great.
The ships sail upon its surface,
   And created whales play in its depths.
All sea creatures at the proper time
   Are fed by Your gracious hand.
They gather the food You give to them,
   They are filled by Your open hand.
They are troubled when Your provision is gone,
   When they have no breath, they die and return to dust.
New life is born when You send Your Spirit,
   This way You continually renew the living of the earth.

May Your glory endure forever,
   May You rejoice in all You created.
You look at the earth and it trembles,
   The mountains smoke when You touch them.
They will always sing praises to You, O Lord;
   I will sing praises to You as long as I live.
Be pleased with all my thoughts about You,
   Because I rejoice in You, O Lord.
May sinners vanish from the face of the earth,
   And the wicked completely disappear.
I praise You, Lord, from the bottom of my soul;
                           Hallelujah.

PSALM 105

A Prayer To Remember God's Deliverance From Egypt

I give thanks to You, O Lord;
   I call on Your name;
   I tell people what You have done.

I sing to You, O Lord;

    I sing praises to You,

    I tell the world Your wonderful acts.

I glory in Your holy name,

    My heart rejoices as I seek You.

I seek Your strength, O Lord;

    I will always seek Your face.

I remember Your wonderful miracles,

    The marvelous things You have done.

I want the seed of Abraham to remember

    Your chosen children of Jacob,

That You are the Lord our God;

    Your decisions are seen everywhere in the earth.

You remember the covenant You made,

    Your Word will continue for a thousand generations.

You made a covenant with Abraham,

    Then You swore it to Isaac.

You next confirmed it to Jacob

    That You would keep it with Israel forever.

You promised to give them the land of Israel,

    As their portion for an inheritance.

It was when they were few in numbers,

    And they were strangers in the land;

They were wandering from one nation to another,

    From one kingdom to another.

You allowed no one to oppose them,

    To protect them, You rebuked kings.

You told them, "Touch not Mine anointed

    And do not harm My prophets."

You sent a famine on the land,

    To destroy all Your people's supply of food.

You sent a man to save them,

    Even Joseph whom they sold as a servant.

His feet were bruised in shackles,

    His neck was put in irons.

Then Joseph foretold what was to come to pass,

    And the word he heard from the Lord was true.

The King sent and released Joseph,

    The rulers of the people set him free.

Joseph was made manager of the King's house,

    And administrator of the food of the land.

He commanded the princes what to do,

    He shared his wisdom with the elders.

His father Jacob was brought to Egypt,

    And he stayed there until he died.

You made Your people grow in number,

    And they became too numerous for the Egyptians.

You turned the hearts of the Egyptians against Israel,

    They put Your people in slavery.

You raised up Moses as their leader,

    And Aaron was chosen to serve with him.

They did miracles for the Egyptians,

    And showed Your wonders to all the people.

You sent darkness, making the land night;

    Because they had rebelled against Your Word.

You turned their water into blood,

    And all the fish died.

You sent frogs into every place in Egypt,

    They even ended up in the rulers' bedrooms.

Then You spoke and flies appeared everywhere,
    Then gnats covered the land.
You made the hail come down like rain,
    And the lightning flashed throughout the land.
The hail stripped the vines of their leaves,
    And destroyed their fruit crop and the trees.
You spoke and the locusts came,
    The grasshoppers couldn't be counted.
They ate all the leaves that were left,
    And devoured all the crops.
You struck down the firstborn in every family,
    The heir in each family.

You brought Your people out of Egypt,
    They were given silver and gold;
    And not one of Your people was sick.
Egypt was glad to see Israel leave,
    Because they were afraid of what might happen.
You spread out a cloud to lead them by day,
    And You gave fire to lead them by night.
You gave them quail when they asked for food,
    And You fed them with bread from Heaven.
You opened the rock for water to gush out,
    It flowed like a river in the desert.
You remembered Your holy promise,
    That You had made to Your servant Abraham.
You brought Your people out of Egypt,
    With rejoicing and shouts of joy.
You gave them the land that had been occupied by the heathen,
    And Your people inherited what others built.
So that they might keep Your laws

And observe Your commandments,

I praise You, Lord.

Amen

PSALM 106

A Prayer To Recount God's Faithfulness And Remember Man's Failure

O Lord, I praise You;

I give thanks to You, O Lord.

For You are good,

Your mercy endureth forever.

No one can fully proclaim Your mighty acts,

No one can fully give You praise.

Lord, You bless those who live justly,

And those who do rightly at all times.

Remember me when You show favor to Your people,

Visit me when You come to save them.

I want to enjoy the goodness of Your chosen ones,

I want to share in the joy of Your people;

I want to join with Your inheritance to praise You.

We have sinned just as did our fathers,

We have done wrong and committed transgressions.

Our fathers did not understand Your miracles in Egypt,

They did not remember Your mercy to them;

And they doubted You could open the Red Sea.

But You delivered them for Your name's sake,

And You made Your power known.

You spoke to the Red Sea and it retreated,
      You led them across on sandy ground.

You saved them from the attack of Pharaoh,
      And redeemed them from their enemy.
The waters covered the Egyptians,
      Not one of them survived.
Then Your people believed Your promise,
      And they sang praises to You.

But Your people soon forgot what You did for them,
      They did not obey Your orders.
The lusted to fill their fleshly appetites,
      In the desert they tempted God.
You gave them what they asked for,
      But sent leanness to the soul.

They complained about Moses' leadership,
      And about Aaron who was consecrated by You.
The earth opened up to swallow Dathan,
      It also buried Abiram.
Fire swept through their camp,
      Burning up the rebels with them.

They made a golden calf at Mount Horeb,
      And worshipped it as an idol.
They quit worshipping Your glory,
      And began worshipping the image of a bull that eats grass.
They forgot that You were their God
      Who had done miracles for them in Egypt,
      And had delivered them through the Red Sea.

So You decided to destroy them,

> But Moses stood in the breech as an intercessor;
> So You would not consume them.

Then they despised the land You gave them,

> They doubted Your promises to them.

They murmured in their tents,

> And would not obey Your voice.

So You swore that they would die in the desert,

> And be scattered throughout the lands.

They joined themselves to Baal,

> And ate sacrifices to the lifeless idol.

They provoked You to anger by their sin,

> And a plague spread throughout their camp.

Then Phinehas acted righteously to intervene,

> And the plague was stopped.

You counted this to him for righteousness,

> So that future generations might take note.

They angered You at the waters of Meribah,

> And Moses paid the consequences for it.

For when the people rebelled against You,

> Moses was judged for speaking ill advisedly.

They did not destroy the inhabitants of the land,

> As You had commanded them to do.

But they mingled with the heathen,

> And began living like them.

Then they worshipped the idols of the land,

> Which became a snare to them.

They sacrificed their sons and daughters to demons,

Shedding the innocent blood of their children;

And the nation was corrupted by their idol-worship.

They defiled themselves by their idolatry,

And became whores to evil practices.

No wonder You were angry with them,

And were disgusted with Your inheritance.

You allowed heathen nations to defeat them,

And their enemies ruled over them.

Their rulers oppressed them,

And forced Your people to serve them.

Many times You delivered them from their enemies,

But they were determined to rebel;

And they were destroyed by their sin.

But You remembered Your covenant with them,

When they cried out to You.

You saw their distress and showed them mercy,

You made their oppressors pity them.

May Israel say, "Save us, O Lord, our God;

Bring us back from the nations

So that we may give thanks to Your name;

And give glory to You in praise."

Lord, I praise You, the God of Israel;

From everlasting to everlasting let the people say

Amen!

PSALM 107

A Prayer To Remind You Of God's Punishment
When You Rebel And His Blessing When You Obey

I give You thanks, O Lord;
　For You are good.
Let the redeemed speak for You,
　Those You have saved from the enemy.
You have gathered them from all lands,
　From the east and the west, from the north and the south.

They wandered lonely in the deserts,
　Not finding a city where they could settle down.
They were hungry and thirsty,
　And their soul fainted within them.
They cried unto You in their trouble,
　And You delivered them out of their distress.

You led them by their right hand,
　To a city where they could settle down.
Oh that all people would praise You,
　For Your goodness and wonderful works to them.
Because You satisfy the thirsty soul,
　And You fill the hungry with good things.

Some sat blinded in the shadow of death,
　They were bound in affliction and sin;
Because they rebelled against Your words,
　And hated Your advice, O Most High.
So You left them bound in misery,
　No one was able to help them out of their bondage.

Then they cried unto You in their trouble,
    And You saved them out of their distress.
You brought them out of the shadow of death,
    And freed them from their chains.
Now let them give thanks for Your goodness,
    And for the wonderful things You do for people.

For You break the prison doors that enslave them,
    And cut through the iron bars that bind them up.
They became fools by their transgressions,
    And suffered because of their iniquities.
They didn't want to eat anything,
    And almost entered the gates of death.

Then they cried unto You in their trouble,
    And You saved them out of their distress.
You sent Your Word to heal them,
    You rescued them from destruction.
Oh that all people would praise You
    For Your goodness and wonderful works to them,
And sacrifice thank offerings to You
    And declare Your works with praise songs.

Those that go out on the sea in ships
    And do their work in the great waters,
They have seen Your wonderful works
    And the things You have done in the deep.
For You spoke and a mighty storm arose,
    That lifted up the powerful waves.
They ride them up high to the heavens,
    They ride them deep into the heart of the ocean;
    They are scared to death because of the storm.

They reel and stagger like a drunken man,
    They don't know what to do.

Then Your people cried unto You in their trouble,
    And You saved them out of their distress.
You quieted the storm to a gentle breeze,
    So that the roaring waves were stilled.
Then they were glad when the wind blew lightly,
    And You led them to their desired port.
Oh that all people would praise You
    For Your goodness and wonderful works to them.

Let them give You thanks in the congregation,
    And praise You in the assembly of the elders.
Because of the wickedness of those in the land,
    A fruitful place became barren.
You turn rivers into a desert,
    And flowing springs into dry ground.
You can also turn the wilderness into wetlands,
    And pour water on dry sandy soil.

You can bring the hungry to live there,
    So they can build a city to live in.
They can plant their fields and vineyards
    That will yield an abundant harvest.
You can bless them and increase their number,
    And not let their herds diminish.

But they can also decrease and become weak,
    When they choose affliction, opposition, and sorrow.
You can humble the proud rulers,
    You can let them wander lost in the wilderness.

But You establish the humble on high,
   And increase their family like flocks.
The righteous see what You do and rejoice,
   But the wicked refuse to acknowledge You.
Those who are wise observe these things,
   They understand the loving way You do things.

Amen

PSALM 108

*A Prayer For Divine Help In Battle**

My heart is fixed, O God;
   I will sing to You with all my heart.
I will awake early to praise You,
   I will awaken to the harp and guitar to do it.
I will praise You among the people, O Lord;
   I will sing to You among the unsaved.
For Your love is great, higher than the heavens;
   And Your faithfulness reaches to the clouds.
I exalt You, O God, above the skies;
   Let Your glory spread over all the earth.

Come and save me with Your right hand,
   Deliver those You love.
You have spoken in Your sanctuary,
   You appointed Shechem and the valley of Succoth.
Gilead and Manasseh are Yours,
   Ephraim is Your crown, Judah Your scepter.
You tossed out Moab and wiped Your feet on Edom,
   You conquered Philistia.

Who will bring me into a secure city,

 And who will lead me in victory over Moab?

Will You not do it for us, O Lord;

 You who rejected us because of our sin,

 You who no longer fight with our armies?

Help us in our struggle with the enemy,

 For human help is not enough.

With You, O God, we will do valiantly;

 For You will stomp upon our enemies.

Amen

*A song or Psalm of David.

HOW TO PRAY

When You Are Angry: The Imprecatory Psalms

There are several Psalms that express judgment and punishment on the enemies of the Psalmist. The writer is praying for his enemies to be punished, killed, or even thrown into hell. The word *imprecatory* means judgment, i.e., a prayer for God to judge His enemies. Most everyone has these human feelings when another attacks them, and most everyone, at one time or another, wants to "get even" with those who hurt them. *Lord, purify my motives.*

But there is a moral question. Can a Christian pray for punishment upon another person? Is it morally justified by the standards of Jesus and the teachings on the Mount to ask God to punish another person, or even to cast them into hell? Where is love, and where is "forgive one another, as I have forgiven you" (see Eph. 4:32)? While there are many imprecatory Psalms, a few of them are more vengeful than others, i.e., 2, 37, 69, 70, 109, and 143.

First of all, realize that these passages are not just the expressions of human anger, but rather "all Scripture is given by inspiration of God" (2 Tim. 3:16). While the individual may have expressed these deep feelings, God inspired them and included them in the Bible. So, we have to determine, why does God include imprecatory Psalms in Scripture when they express such dark and negative feelings?

The Psalmist is never just praying for punishment, but rather these Psalms show his zeal and passion for God's cause. In most cases, these Psalms are battle cries. Someone is trying to kill the speaker. Swords are drawn and arrows are flying. Blood is flowing. The Psalmist prays against an enemy who is trying to kill him because the enemy hates holiness, despises God, and is an enemy of the Psalmist. The enemy is trying to destroy the cause of God and people of God. *Lord, defend me when my battle comes.*

Also, the Psalmist is praying for God Himself to administer punishment. These Psalms are not prayers for personal revenge, but rather a willingness by the Psalmist to leave revenge in the hands of God.

On another side, these Psalms show the continuing battle between God and satan, a conflict between Heaven and hell. That conflict is being raged in the life of every believer, so every believer can pray these imprecatory Psalms in relationship to the devil and his demons. Remember, satan hates God's covenant people, the Jews, just as much as he hates God's people, the Church. *Lord, defend me from my enemy.*

As you pray judgment upon your enemies, remember you must do it for the right motive, i.e., these people hate God. Your prayer is not about yourself, but about God. Because God says, "I the Lord thy God am a jealous God, visiting the iniquity of the fathers upon the children unto the third and fourth generation of them that hate Me" (Ex. 20:5 KJV). Did you see that qualifying statement in that passage? It's about "them that hate Me." If God will punish them, how can we pray otherwise?

But, Jesus taught us to pray the Lord's Prayer, i.e., "And forgive us our debts, as we forgive our debtors" (Mt. 6:12). That means we must first personally forgive our enemies, even knowing God will judge them. In another place Jesus said, "Love your enemies. Do good to them who hate you. Bless them that curse you, and pray for them which despitefully use you" (Lk. 6:27-28 KJV). That means you must have a forgiving spirit when you pray for your enemies. When you "bless them" and "pray for them which despitefully use you," your heart must be right with God and you must want them converted.

However, there is a flipside to blessing your enemies. Paul tells us that by praying for our enemies, certain actions take place. You must "avenge not yourselves, but rather give place unto wrath" (Rom. 12:19 KJV). Why must you not "get even with your enemies"? Because it is written, "Vengeance is Mine; I [God] will repay, saith the Lord" (Rom. 12:19). And if you give your enemy food, and drink, and pray for them; what happens? "For in so doing thou shalt heap coals of fire on his head" (Romans 12:20 KJV). Therefore by blessing your enemies, the reverse happens. If they refuse the blessing of God, He judges them.

Therefore in the Old Testament, the Psalmist prayed judgment on his enemies. In the New Testament Jesus said bless your enemies. Should your enemies reject God's blessing, He will pour coals of fire on their head. Therefore, there is no difference in results between the imprecatory Psalms of the Old Testament, and the teachings of Jesus in the Sermon on the Mount. While Jesus focused on the attitude in the heart, the imprecatory

Psalms focus on the end result. *Lord, I don't pray for judgment on my enemies. I pray for Your blessings on them.*

Imprecatory Psalms

PSALM 2:   THE LORD'S WRATH

PSALM 7:   THE LORD IS JUST

PSALM 35:   PRAYER FOR VINDICATION

PSALM 37:   DELIGHT IN THE LORD

PSALM 55:   BETRAYED BY A FRIEND

PSALM 58:   VENGANCE OF THE LORD

PSALM 59:   PRAYER FOR DELIVERANCE

PSALM 69:   URGENT PLEA FOR HELP

PSALM 70:   THE LORD MY DELIVERER

PSALM 79:   PRAYER FOR RESTORATION

PSALM 82:   DEFEND THE POOR

PSALM 83:   THE ENEMIES OF THE RIGHTEOUS

PSALM 88:   A PRAYER OF THE AFFLICTED

PSALM 94:   VENGEANCE BELONGS TO GOD

PSALM 109:   JUDGMENT ON FALSE ACCUSERS

PSALM 137:   REMEMBER ZION

PSALM 139:   GOD KNOWS US INTIMATELY

PSALM 140:   PRAYER FOR PRESERVATION

PSALM 143:   PRAYER FOR GUIDANCE

PSALM 109

*A Prayer Of Judgment On Your Enemies For Persecuting You**

O God, I praise You;

Do not keep silent when I need You.

The wicked, deceitful enemy attacks me,
  He is lying about me.
He hates everything I do,
  And he opposes me for no reason at all.
He returned evil when I gave him my friendship,
  Now I can do nothing but pray about it.
He has rewarded my good with evil,
  He hated the love I showed to him.

Raise up the evil person to oppose him,
  Let satan the accuser stand at his right hand.
Judge him and declare him guilty,
  And may his cry for mercy condemn him.
Let his days be few,
  And let someone else take his place.
Let his children be fatherless,
  And let his wife be a widow.
May his children be wandering street people,
  Drive them desolate from their homes.
May the creditors seize all his assets,
  And may looters plunder all he has left.
Don't let anyone show him mercy,
  Nor extend help to his children.
May his descendants be destroyed,
  And may his family name be terminated.
May the iniquity of his father be remembered before You, Lord;
  May the sins of his mother never be forgiven.
Always remember his sin, O Lord;
  But don't let anyone on earth remember that he ever lived.

My enemy didn't show mercy to the poor,
  But tormented continuously the needy and discouraged.

He loved to curse, so curse him continuously;
    He hated to bless, so don't bless him.
He covered himself with vile language;
    He drank it in like water.
May his swearing words choke him like a scarf,
    May his filthy speech squeeze him like a tight belt.
Let all this be my adversary's reward,
    Because he cursed me as I lived for You.

But You, Lord God, have been good to me;
    For Your name's sake You have delivered me,
    You have shown Your goodness and love to me.
I am defenseless and needy,
    All hope in my heart had collapsed.
I was fading away like the evening shadows,
    I was shaken like a grasshopper in the storm.
I was weak because of fasting for answers,
    And my body was emaciated and anemic.
Everyone was ridiculing me,
    They shook their heads in disbelief when they saw me.

Help me, O Lord, God;
    Save me by Your mercy.
May they see Your hand working in my life,
    And understand what You have done for me.
They may curse me, but You bless me;
    Put them to shame when they attack me,
    But let me rejoice in Your presence.
Wrap them in the coats of embarrassment,
    And cover them with disgrace.

I will worship You with my mouth,

I will praise You among the congregation.

For You stand at the right hand of this needy person,

To protect me from the condemnation of my enemy.

Amen

*A Psalm of David.

PSALM 110

*A Prayer For The Lord To Judge Those Who Oppose Jesus**

Lord, You said to Jesus;

To come sit at Your right hand,

While You put His enemies under Your feet.

Lord, You extended Your powerful scepter out from Zion;

To rule over all Your enemies.

Your people will serve You in the day of battle,

They will be beautifully dressed in holiness;

To serve You from the dawn of the morning,

Until the dew finishes the day.

Lord, You have vowed and will not change Your mind;

That Jesus will be a Priest forever;

He serves according to the order of Melchizedek.

Lord, You will be at the right hand of Jesus;

To crush the kings that oppose Him.

Jesus will judge all the nations,

Those who rebel will die;

The rulers of great countries will be destroyed.

He will drink from the brook after the task,

His head will be exalted in victory.

Amen

*A Psalm of David.

PSALM 111

A Prayer Of Thanksgiving Because You Understand And Follow God's Principles

I praise You, Lord;

    I magnify You with all my heart.

I praise You, Lord;

    In the assembly of true worshippers.

Great are Your works, O Lord;

    I meditate on them with other worshippers.

You do things gloriously and majestically,

    Your righteousness never fails.

I cannot forget the wonders You do,

    You are gracious and merciful to me.

You give food to those who trust You,

    Who always live by the principles You gave us.

You have displayed Your great power to us,

    Giving us the land of other people.

All You do is just and good,

    I confidently live by all Your principles.

Your truth is forever trustworthy,

    You gave it to us in Your integrity.

You redeemed Your people,

    You guaranteed to keep us forever;

    Holy and revered is Your name,

    I begin to understand true wisdom.

All who live by Your principles

Are rewarded by true wisdom.

Praise Your name forever.

Amen

PSALM 112

A Prayer For A Godly Testimony

Lord, I praise You;

For blessing me when I fear You,

For blessing me when I delight in Your Word.

You have promised my children will be influential,

You will bless them when they do right.

You have promised to bless me with wealth and riches,

When I continually live righteously.

Help me to be upright as a light in darkness,

And to be gracious and compassionate to all.

Lord, help me graciously give to the needy;

And guide my life with truth.

Then I shall not be shaken,

And my righteousness will be remembered forever.

Lord, I will not be afraid of bad news;

Help me to be steadfast in trusting You.

Help me to be established and not afraid,

And let me triumph over my enemies.

Lord, I want to give to the poor;

I want my testimony to endure forever,

I want You to honor me.

Let my wicked enemies see it,

And be terrified of coming judgment.

Let them gnash their teeth in fear,

To realize they will perish.

Amen

PSALM 113

A Prayer Of Praise To God

Lord, I praise Your holy name;

I come to praise You with Your servants.

Lord, I bless Your name;

I bless You both now and forever.

From the rising of the sun until its going down,

I praise Your name, O Lord.

You are exalted above the nations, O Lord;

Your glory is above the heavens.

Who can be compared to You our Lord and God,

You sit on Your throne.

You descend to examine the affairs

On both the Heaven and earth.

You lift up the poor from the ground

And raise the needy from despair.

You set them among the honored ones,

Even among the leaders of their people.

You give a home to the woman without children

So she can be a mother;

Lord, I praise You.

     Amen

PSALM 114

A Prayer That Recognizes
The Power Of God's Presence

Lord, You dwelt in Israel as Your sanctuary;

     When the nation left Egypt.

You made the house of Jacob Your dominion,

     When Your people left those speaking a strange language.

The Red Sea saw You coming,

     And parted for Israel to cross.

The Jordan River acknowledged Your presence,

     And the waters rolled back.

The mountains skipped like happy rams,

     And the hills play like little lambs.

Why did this happen, that the Red Sea parted,

     And that the Jordan backed up?

Why did the mountains skip like rams,

     And the little hills played like lambs?

Because of Your presence, O Lord;

     Let the earth tremble when You come near.

You brought pools of water from the Rock of Meribah,

     Water poured out from a solid rock.

     Amen

PSALM 115

A Prayer Of Praise To God
For Life And Blessing

Not to me, O Lord, goes the glory;
  But I glorify You because of Your name.
Not to me goes glory,
  But to You because of Your mercy and truth.
Why are the heathen asking,
  "Where is the God of His followers?"
For You, O God, are in the heavens;
  You do whatever You want to do.

Their gods are nothing but silver and gold idols,
  The workmanship of their hands.
They have mouths, but cannot speak;
  Eyes have they, but cannot see.
They have ears, but they cannot hear;
  Noses have they, but cannot smell.
They have hands, but they cannot handle;
  Feet have they, but cannot walk;
  Nor can they speak intelligently.
Those who create idols, make them like themselves,
  And those who trust idols, are only worshipping themselves.

Israel must trust in You, Lord;
  For You are their help and protection.
The priest must trust in You, Lord;
  For You are their help and protection.
All those who acknowledge You, Lord;
  Must trust You for help and protection.

Lord, remember and bless us accordingly;

Bless the house of Israel,

And bless the priests who serve You.

Bless all those who acknowledge You,

Bless small and great alike.

Lord, prosper my life with Your blessing;

Both me and my children.

May I be blessed by You, O Lord;

Maker of Heaven and earth.

The highest Heaven belongs to You, O Lord;

But You have given the earth to us.

The dead cannot sing praises to You, O Lord;

For they are silent in the grave.

We the living bless You, O Lord;

From this time into eternity,

I praise You, O Lord.

Amen

PSALM 116

A Prayer Of Gratitude After God Delivers You From Trouble

I love You, Lord,

Because You heard and answered my prayer.

Because You listened to me,

I will pray to You as long as I live.

I was scared to death,

And thought I was going to die;

I was so worried I couldn't think straight.

Then I called on You, O Lord;
"Please come and save me."

Lord, You are gracious and kind.
    You were merciful to me.
Lord, You protect those with simple faith;
    When I was in trouble, You saved me.
Once again I am peaceful,
    Because You have been good to me.
You kept me from dying,
    And I no longer cry.

So now I walk in Your presence,
    Among the land of the living.
Because I believe in You,
    I told You all my trouble.
When I was upset I complained to You,
    That all men are liars.
What can I do for You, Lord;
    For all You have done for me?
All I can do is drink from Your cup of salvation,
    And praise Your name for saving me.

I will keep my promises to You, O Lord;
    In the presence of Your people.
The ones who are faithful to the end,
    Are precious to You when they die.
O Lord, I am Your servant, the son of Your handmaid;
    You have given me freedom in serving You.

I will worship You with the sacrifice of thanksgiving,
    And call upon Your name, O Lord.

I will keep my promises to You, O Lord;
In the presence of Your people,
In the heart of Jerusalem.
In the courts of Your house,
Praise Your name, O Lord.

Amen

PSALM 117

A Prayer Of Praise From All People

We praise You, Lord, with the different ethnic groups of the earth;
We praise You with all people of the earth,
For You love us with unending love;
Your faithfulness endures forever.
We praise You, Lord.

Amen

PSALM 118

A Prayer Of Gratitude To God For Victory And Salvation

I give thanks to You, Lord,
For You are good and Your love endures forever.
I join all Your people to proclaim,
Your love endures forever.
I join the priests of Aaron to proclaim,
Your love endures forever.
I join all who fear You to proclaim,
Your love endures forever.

In my trouble, I called on You, Lord;
    You answered me and delivered me.
Lord, You are with me, I will not fear;
    What can anyone do to me?
Lord, You are with me, and will help me;
    I will triumph over my enemies.
I know it is better to put my trust in You,
    Than to put my confidence in anyone on earth.
I know it is better to put my trust in You,
    Than to put my confidence in human leaders.

Though hostile enemies surround me,
    I will defeat them in Your name.
Even when my enemies have me hemmed in,
    I will defeat them in Your name.
They may swarm around me like bees,
    They may circle around me like fire in dead thorn bushes;
    But I will defeat them in Your name.

I retreated and was almost defeated,
    But You helped me, O Lord.
You are the strength of my battle, O Lord;
    I sing of You in my victory song.
Shouts of joy and victorious songs of praise,
    Are sung among those who have been redeemed.

Your mighty right arm has done glorious things,
    Your mighty right arm has been exalted.
I will not be defeated but I will live,
    And I will tell what You have done for me.
You punished me severely for my sin,
    But You did not deliver me to death.

Open the gates of righteousness for me,

    And I will enter to give thanks to You, O Lord.

Open the gates that lead to Your presence,

    And the godly will come in to You.

Thank You for answering my prayers,

    And for saving me from my troubles.

The stone which the builders rejected,

    Has now become the cornerstone of the building.

You have accomplished this great thing,

    And it is a marvelous thing to see.

This is the day that You have made,

    I will rejoice in it and be glad.

And now, O Lord, please save me;

    And please give me success, O Lord.

Bless the one who comes in Your name,

    Bless him because of the One standing in Your presence.

Lord, You have accepted me into Your light;

    I bring the sacrifice to Your altar.

You are my God, and I offer You thanks;

    You are my God, and I exalt You.

I give thanks to You, Lord;

    For You are good, and Your love endures forever.

                               Amen

PSALM 119

A Prayer For God To Use His Word In Your Life

a
ALEPH

Lord, You bless those who are blameless;
  Who walk according to Your law.
You bless those who keep Your statutes,
  And seek You with all their hearts.
They do not commit iniquity,
  But they walk according to Your way.
You have commanded us to keep Your precepts,
  Oh that I was steadfast in doing it.
Then I would not be shamed,
  Because I respected all Your commandments.
I will praise You with the integrity of my heart,
  As I continue learning that Your laws are right.
I will obey Your statutes,
  Do not ever leave me.

b
BETH

How can a young man keep clean?
  By knowing and obeying Your Word.
I seek You with my whole heart,
  Never let me stray from Your commandments.
Your Word have I hid in my heart,
  That I might not sin against You.
I praise You, Lord; help me understand Your Word;
  My lips repeat the laws You gave to us.
I am happy when I follow Your testimonies,

As one that rejoices in riches.
I will meditate on Your precepts,
    And respect the way I'm to live.
I delight in Your statutes,
    And will not forget Your Word.

g
GIMEL

Bless me so I may live before You,
    And keep the Word You have given.
Open my eyes so I can see
    Wonderful truths in Your law.
I am a stranger on earth,
    Do not withhold Your Word from me;
    My soul is always longing for Your laws.
You rebuke the rebellious who are cursed,
    Because they wander from Your commandments.
Take away my scorn and contempt,
    Because I follow Your testimonies.
Although rulers agree to condemn me,
    I will meditate on Your statutes.
Your testimonies are my delight,
    They guide me in the way I should live.

d
DALETH

When I am crushed into the dust,
    Revive me with Your Word.
You heard how I testified about Your way,
    Teach me more of Your Word to do it again.
Make me understand what Your precepts mean,

So I can tell others of Your wonderful way.
My soul is burdened down with worry,
Lift me up with Your Word.
Keep me from being deceitful,
And help me keep Your law.
I have chosen to tell the truth,
Your judgments will be my standard.
I will hold on to the expectations of Your law,
Lord, don't let me change my commitment.
I run to keep Your commandments,
For You have given me a new heart to do it.

h
HE

Teach me, O Lord, to follow Your statutes;
And I will always obey them.
Help me understand Your law,
And I will wholeheartedly observe it.
Make me follow Your commandments,
And I will find delight in them.
Incline my heart toward Your testimonies,
So I won't be selfishly greedy.
Turn my eyes away from looking at vain attractions,
Renew my life with Your words.
Fulfill Your Scriptures to me,
So that I may worship You in awe.
Take away the things I fear,
And give me Your good judgments.
Because I long to know Your precepts,
Revive my desire to be righteous.

ᴡ
WAW

Show me Your daily mercies, O Lord;
>   Save me according to the promises of Your Word.
Then I can answer the one criticizing me,
>   For I trust the answers in Your Word.
Do not take Your truth out of my life,
>   For I put my trust in it.
I will always obey Your law,
>   And will enjoy the freedom it gives me.
I will testify Your truth before kings,
>   I will not be intimidated by them.
I will constantly delight in Your commandments,
>   Because I love them.
I will lift up Your commandments with my hand,
>   And will meditate on them constantly.

ᴢ
ZAYIN

Remember the Word You have given to me,
>   Because I have put my trust in it.
I take comfort in what You have said,
>   Because Your Word gives me hope.
My enemies mock me for trusting You,
>   But I have not turned away from Your love.
I remember the laws You originally gave,
>   And I still trust in them.
I am angry at the wicked,
>   Because they have forsaken Your law.
I can't help singing about Your words,
>   They are my theme song wherever I live.

In the night I meditate on Your name, O Lord;

Because it helps me keep Your commandments.

My practice through the years has been

To obey all the precepts of Your law.

j

HETH

You are my portion, O Lord;

I promise to obey Your law.

I have sought Your face with all my strength,

Mercifully answer me according to Your promise.

When I examined my ways,

I began walking according to Your statutes.

So I will act on Your commandments quickly,

And not delay my obedience.

Even when my enemies tie me up and rob me,

I will always respond according to Your law.

At midnight I wake up to give You thanks,

For Your laws make me live right.

I will be a friend to all who fear You,

And who follow Your precepts.

The earth is filled with Your love,

Teach me to live by Your expectations.

v

TETH

Lord, You have done good things to me;

Just as You promised in Your Word.

Teach me good judgment and knowledge,

For I believe wisdom is found in Your commands.

Before You disciplined me, I strayed from You;

But now I know to keep Your Word.

You are good and You only do good things,

   Teach me Your principles to live by.

My enemies have told lies about me,

   But I keep Your precepts in my heart.

Their heart is blind and disobedient

   To the truth that I keep.

It was good for me to be in trouble,

   Because I learned Your statutes.

The law spoken by You is better

   Than thousands of gold and silver coins.

y
YODH

You made me with Your hands,

   Now give me discernment to learn Your commandments.

May all who fear You rejoice when they see me,

   Because I too have put my trust in You.

I know that Your decisions are fair,

   And You punished me because I deserved it.

Now comfort me with Your merciful kindness,

   As You promised to do in Your Word.

Cover me with Your tender mercies so that I may live,

   For I find happiness in Your law.

May my enemies be embarrassed for telling lies about me,

   But I will meditate on Your commandments.

I want to be reconciled with those who fear You,

   And those who know Your testimonies.

May I blamelessly keep Your commandments,

   Then I'll never be embarrassed.

k
KAPH

I thought I wasn't going to be saved,
　　But my trust in Your Word strengthened me.
I had difficulty seeing Your Word,
　　When will You encourage me?
I was empty like a bottle of smoke,
　　So I hung on to Your promises.
I don't know how long I will live,
　　So I want You to judge my persecutors.
My enemies have tried to trip me up,
　　They don't live by Your laws.
All the promises You gave me will work,
　　So help me respond properly to my enemies.
They have almost overcome me,
　　But I still hang on to Your Word.
Give me new life through Your Word,
　　And I will obey Your commandments.

m
LAMEDH

Lord, Your Word is forever settled in Heaven;
　　You are faithful to all generations,
　　You established the abiding earth.
Your promises continue to this day,
　　And are applied to all Your followers.
Without the encouragement of Your law,
　　I would have given in to my affliction.
I will never forsake Your Word,
　　For it gives me life and hope.
I am Your servant and belong to You,
　　I will always seek and follow Your Scripture.

The wicked are waiting to destroy me,

But I will still look for Your precepts.

I have seen every perfect thing cease,

But Your commands will reach everywhere.

ל
MEM

O Lord, I love Your law;

I meditate on it all day long.

Your commandments make me wiser than my enemies,

For they are my constant guide.

I get more understanding from Your law than from my teachers,

Because I constantly think about Your commandments.

I am even wiser than my elders,

Because I obey Your precepts.

I have refused to follow evil paths,

Because they disagree with Your Word.

I have not neglected Your standards,

For they have profited my life.

Your words are sweet to my taste,

Sweeter than my favorite dessert.

I gain understanding from Your commandments,

Therefore I hate everything that takes me away from You.

נ
NUN

Your Word is a light for my feet,

You help me see the path in the dark.

I have taken an oath to obey

The wonderful command You gave me.

Because I've suffered much, revive me;

Because You promised to do it, O Lord.
I give You an offering of praise,
   So teach me how to do it better.
I bring my soul in my hands to You,
   Just as You teach me to do in Your law.
My enemies have tried to trip me up,
   But I will not depart from Your standards.
The stories of Your exploits are my heritage,
   I get excited when I read about them.
My heart is committed to keep Your law,
   To the very end of my life.

s
SAMEKH

I hate those who claim to love You, but disobey You;
   But as for me, I love Your Word.
You are my defender and shield,
   Therefore, I trust what You tell me.
I don't want evildoers anywhere near me,
   Because I keep Your commandments, O God.
Hold me steadily by Your Word,
   And I will put my trust in You.
You reject all who have rejected Your statutes,
   But I cling to Your loving ways.
I would be afraid not to obey You,
   Because I fear Your judgments.

y
AYIN

I have done the right thing in the right way,
   Do not leave me to my enemies.

Guarantee my spiritual wealth and blessing,

    Don't let the oppressor tear me down.

My eyes strain to see Your salvation,

    I'm looking for Your righteous Word.

Deal with me by Your mercy,

    And teach me the meaning of Your statutes.

Give me discernment for I am Your servant,

    Then will I understand Your will.

Lord, now is the time for You to act;

    They are breaking Your law.

You know I love Your commandments better than gold,

    I love them more than pure gold.

And because I know all Your precepts are right,

    I hate everything that is false.

p
PE

Your statutes are wonderful,

    Therefore, I love to obey them.

I get understanding when I read Your Word,

    Even average people get insight from it.

I open my mouth to receive Your Scriptures,

    Because I long to know what You say.

Come show me Your love and faithfulness,

    As You do to those who love Your name.

Guide me by Your words,

    And don't let sin control me.

Deliver me from my oppressing enemy,

    So I can obey Your commandments.

Shine the presence of Your face on me,

    And teach me how to live by Your law.

I can't help the tears running down my face,
  Because people disobey Your law.

x
TSDAHE

You are always doing the right thing, O Lord;
  And Your decisions are right.
Your directions are the right thing for us,
  I can fully trust them with my soul.
I am overcome with anger,
  Because my enemies won't obey Your commands.
Your words are absolutely honest,
  Therefore I love everything about it.
Though I am insignificant and despised,
  I have not forgotten Your precepts.
Your righteousness is as eternal as You are,
  And Your law is absolutely true.
When trouble and anxiety overwhelm me,
  Your commandments get me through problems.
Your testimonies are always right,
  Help me to understand them and live.

q
KOPH

Answer me, when I call to You with all my heart;
  I will continue obeying Your laws.
I again call out for You to save me,
  I will continue obeying Your statutes.
I get up early in the morning to cry for help,
  I will continue to put my trust in Your Word.
I remain awake through the different hours of the night,

Meditating on the promises of Your Word.

Hear my request because You promised to do it,

    Renew my life by Your Word.

Those who plan to attack me are nearby,

    But I know they live far from You.

Yet You are near to me,

    And I can depend on the truthfulness of Your commands.

I learned when I was very young

    That You established Your commands to last forever.

r

RESH

Look on my pain and deliver me,

    For I have not forgotten Your Word.

Come help me and defend me,

    Deliver me as You have promised.

The wicked are far from being saved,

    They will not seek Your Word.

Your mercy is great, O Lord;

    Revive me according to Your laws.

I have many enemies and oppressors,

    But I have not rejected Your promises.

I am grieved when I see them hate You,

    Because they reject Your Word.

Look how I love Your promises,

    Revive me according to Your Word.

All Your words are true from the beginning,

    Because Your laws are right, they will forever stand.

V
SHIN

Even when rulers persecute me without a cause,

My heart still respects Your Word.

I rejoice in Your Scriptures,

Like someone finding a great treasure.

I hate those who lie,

But I love Your law.

Seven times a day I praise You,

For giving me right laws by which to live.

They who love Your Scripture will have great peace,

Nothing shall offend them.

I have put my hope in Your salvation,

And have obeyed Your laws.

I have obeyed Your commands,

And love them with all my heart.

I have obeyed Your statutes,

You know it, because You know everything.

t
TAW

Listen to my prayer, O Lord;

Help me to understand what is in Your Word.

Listen to my prayer,

Deliver me according to Your promise.

My lips pour out praise to You,

Because You taught me Your Word.

My tongue sings about Your promises,

For they help me live right.

Let Your hand help me,

Because I have chosen to follow Your precepts.

O Lord, I long for Your salvation;

　　Your law gives me happiness.

Let me live so I can praise You,

　　And may Your Scriptures sustain me.

I have strayed like a lost sheep,

　　Come find me;

　　For I have not forgotten Your commandments.

Amen

HOW TO PRAY

The Psalms Of Degrees
(Also Called The Psalms Of Ascent)

The word *degrees* means "steps." There are fifteen Psalms in the Psalms of Degrees (i.e., Psalms 120—134). In Jesus' day, these Psalms were sung by the pilgrims going to the three annual required feasts in Jerusalem (Passover, Pentecost, and Tabernacles). They would sing these Psalms as they climbed the mountains toward Jerusalem. Because of this, they are called "the Psalms of Ascent," as in ascending a mountain.

Some say the title *degrees* began with the exiles returning to Jerusalem from captivity during the reign of Artaxerxes. They sang these Psalms as they approached Jerusalem. Others say these Psalms got their name from the fifteen steps from the court of the women up to the court of the men in the Temple where Levitical singers performed, using these steps as a stage. Some others say the fifteen Psalms were a part of a worship procedure as the priests advanced up these steps in preparation to sacrifice to the Lord. The word *degrees* might mean "step to step" as seen in Psalm 121:4-5; 124:1-4. *Lord, guide my steps as I go from "faith to faith"* (Rom. 1:17).

Still others say that the fifteen Psalms correspond in number with the fifteen years that were added to Hezekiah's life. When Hezekiah prayed to live longer, God increased his years when the shadow of the sun went backwards ten degrees on the sundial of Ahaz (2 Kings 20:8-11). The number of fifteen Psalms corresponds with the number of years (15) that were added to Hezekiah's life. At the same time the number of ten Psalms written by Hezekiah corresponds to the number of degrees by which the "shadow of the sun went backwards."

Solomon's Psalm (127) is the center Psalm with two Psalms by David on each side of the center (a total of four), and ten Psalms written by Hezekiah, i.e., the total number of fifteen Psalms. Also to understand the symmetry of the Psalms of Degree, the name *Jehovah* (Lord) occurs twenty-four times in each of the seven Psalms on either side of the center Psalm, and the name *Jehovah* occurs only three times in the central Psalm. *Lord, teach me Your Word.*

Authorship of the Psalms of Degrees

PSALM 120: BY HEZEKIAH

PSALM 121: BY HEZEKIAH

PSALM 122: BY DAVID

PSALM 123: BY HEZEKIAH

PSALM 124: BY DAVID

PSALM 125: BY HEZEKIAH

PSALM 126: BY HEZEKIAH

PSALM 127: (THE CENTRAL PSALM) BY SOLOMON

PSALM 128: BY HEZEKIAH

PSALM 129: BY HEZEKIAH

PSALM 130: BY HEZEKIAH

PSALM 131: BY DAVID

PSALM 132: BY HEZEKIAH

PSALM 133: BY DAVID

PSALM 134: BY HEZEKIAH

Some ask the question, Why was Hezekiah's name not on the ten Psalms ascribed to him? (Examine the footnotes.) The answer is that all Israel knew these Psalms belonged to Hezekiah. He even called them "my Psalms." When Hezekiah was shut up in Jerusalem by Sennacherib, he trusted Jehovah for victory over his enemies. But he didn't understand how "obsessive" were his enemies. The words of Sennacherib are found on a cylinder that records this campaign in Israel that can be seen in the British Museum, London, England. It says, "I fixed upon him . . . Hezekiah king of the Jews, who had not submitted to my yoke, forty-six of his fenced in cities, and the strongholds, and the small cities which were roundabout them, and which were without number, by the battering of rams, and the attack of engines, and by the assault of foot soldiers and . . . I captured 200,150 people

... horses, and mules, and asses, and camels, and men, and sheep innumerable, and I reckoned ... Hezekiah himself like a caged bird within Jerusalem his royal city I shut in." This historical description perfectly fits the details of the Bible. About this time, Hezekiah became sick and was threatened with death. God sent the prophet Isaiah to tell him he would die. But Hezekiah interceded for God to give him more time. God gave him an extra fifteen years (the number of Psalms of Degrees). Then God delivered Hezekiah from death and delivered him from Sennacherib. Hezekiah expressed gratitude to God for deliverance. As here he writes, "my Psalms." *Lord, just as Hezekiah had "his Psalms," so I claim all the Psalms as "my Psalms," because they express my prayers to You.*

The Lord was ready to save me; therefore we will sing my songs with stringed instruments all the days of our life, in the house of the Lord (Is. 38:20).

PSALM 120

*A Prayer For Peace And Comfort**

I called to You, Lord, when I was in trouble,
    You heard me when I prayed.
Save me, O Lord, from liars;
    And from deceitful people.
God, what will You do to the liars;
    And how much will You punish them?
Inflict them with the pain of sharp arrows,
    And with the torment of burning coals.

I am suffering because I live in Meshech,
    And stay in the tents of Kedar.
I have lived too long
    Among those who hate peace.
I am a lover of peace,
    But they are all men of war.

                    Amen

*A song of degrees.

PSALM 121

*A Prayer Of Appreciation For God's Protection**

I lift up my eyes to the hills,
  But does my help come from there?
No! My help comes from You, Lord;
  You made the heavens and the earth.
Your foot will not stumble,
  Indeed, You who watch over Israel
  Will not get tired, nor will You sleep.
Lord, watch over me to keep me;
  Stand at my right hand to protect me.
The sun will not harm me during the day,
  Nor will the moon at night.
Lord, deliver me from all evil;
  Preserve my soul.
Lord, watch over me as I come and go;
  Both now in this present age and forever more.

Amen

*A song of degrees.

PSALM 122

*A Prayer For Peace In Jerusalem**

I was glad when they said to me,
  Let us go into Your house, O Lord.
Now I am standing inside Your gate,
  I'm standing in Your city of Jerusalem.
Jerusalem is the eternal city,
  It is tightly built together.

This is where the people of Israel come,

    They come here to praise You.

As the commandments instruct,

    They come to worship Your name.

You have put the seat of government here,

    The throne of David rules from this city.

Lord, I pray for the peace of Jerusalem;

    May all prosper who love You.

May there be peace within these walls,

    And prosperity within the palaces.

For the sake of my relatives and friends,

    I pray for peace within this city.

For the sake of Your house, O God;

    I pray for prosperity in Jerusalem.

Amen

*A song of degrees of David.

PSALM 123

*A Prayer For Acceptance By God**

I look up to You, O God;

    As You sit on Your throne in Heaven.

I lift up my eyes to You, O God;

    As the servant looks to the hand of his master,

    As the maid looks to the hand of her mistress.

I look to You, O Lord, my God;

    That You would show me mercy.

Be gracious to me, O Lord, be gracious;

    For I can't stand rejection.

I have been criticized by the proud,

And I have been rejected by the arrogant.

Amen

*A song of degrees.

PSALM 124

*A Prayer Of Gratitude For Deliverance**

If You had not been on my side, Lord;

I tell everyone who will listen.

If You had not been on my side,

When my enemies attacked me;

They would have swallowed me alive,

Because their anger was so hot against me.

The waters would have drowned me,

The torrent would have flooded my soul.

The angry waters from the storm

Would have overwhelmed my life.

I bless You, Lord, for Your protection;

Because You did not let them devour me.

I have escaped like a bird,

Out of the trap of the hunter;

I am free because the trap was broken.

You are my defender, O Lord;

You are the Creator of the heavens and the earth.

Amen

*A song of degrees of David.

PSALM 125

*A Prayer For Peace For The Godly**

Because I trust in You, Lord,

    I am as secure as Mount Zion;

    I will not be shaken, but will abide forever.

Just as the mountains surround Jerusalem

    To give it protection,

    So You, Lord, surround and protect Your people.

The wicked will not rule the godly,

    Lest they make the godly do evil.

O Lord, do good to those who are good;

    To those whose hearts are upright.

But to those who follow crooked ways,

    Expel them with the evil ones.

Give peace to Israel.

                           Amen

*A song of degrees.

PSALM 126

*A Prayer For Renewal**

Lord, when You returned the exiles to Jerusalem;

    It was like I was dreaming.

I laughed with joy,

    And I sang a happy song.

The Gentiles were amazed, saying,

    The Lord has done great things for them.

Yes, You, Lord, have done great things for us all;

    Overflowing our hearts with joy.

O Lord, restore our lives;

    As the streams restore the desert.

Those who plant with tears,

    Will sing heartedly during the harvest.

He who goes out weeping to plant,

    Carrying his seed to sow;

Will come from the work singing for joy,

    Carrying his sheaves with him.

                       Amen

*A song of degrees.

PSALM 127

*A Prayer Of Gratitude For Your Family**

Except You build the family, Lord;

    The work of the workers is useless.

Unless You watch over the city, Lord;

    The watch of the watchman is in vain.

It is useless to toil and work,

    Getting up early and staying up late;

Worrying about getting enough food to eat,

    Because You supply the needs of those You love.

Lord, You give children as a gift;

    The fruit of the womb is Your reward.

Like weapons in the hands of a warrior,

    Are children born to a wise family.

Blessed is the man whose quiver is full,

    Because his children defend him against his accuser.

                       Amen

*A song of degrees for Solomon.

PSALM 128

A Prayer Of Blessing Upon The Home*

Lord, You prosper those who fear You;
  You bless those who follow Your ways.
They enjoy the fruit of their labors,
  You give them happiness and prosperity.
Their wives will be like a fruitful vine,
  Flourishing within their home.
They will have many children
  Sitting around the table,
That is one of the ways You bless
  Those that fear You.

May You bless them from Zion,
  All the days of their life.
May they see the prosperity of Jerusalem,
  As long as they live.
May they live to see their children's children;
  Lord, I pray peace upon Your people.

                                        Amen

*A song of degrees.

PSALM 129

A Prayer Against Your Enemies*

Lord, my enemies have tormented me;
  Ever since I was young.
They have oppressed me as I was growing up,
  But they have not been victorious.

Like a plow on my back,

They have made deep furrows.

But Lord, You have been good to me;

You have freed me from their bondage.

May those who hate Your people

Be defeated and embarrassed.

May they be like grass without roots,

That withers because it can't grow.

May reapers reject them at harvest,

Because they are not good for anything.

May no one passing by bless my enemies,

Nor say, "The blessing of the Lord's name upon them."

Amen

*A song of degrees.

PSALM 130

*A Prayer For Forgiveness And Acceptance**

Out of my depth of trouble,

I call to You, O Lord;

Please listen to my cry for help.

If You kept a record of our sin,

No one could stand before You.

But there is forgiveness with You,

So that we fear You.

I wait for You, Lord;

And I put my trust in Your Word.

I wait for You, Lord;

More than the watchmen wait for the morning.

Let us all put our hope in You, Lord;

For there is loving kindness with You;

And there is redemption in You.

For You will redeem us all

From all our iniquities.

Amen

*A song of degrees.

PSALM 131

*A Prayer Of Communion With God**

Lord, I am not egotistical over who I am;

Nor am I proud of what I do.

I am not concerned about these self-serving ambitions,

Nor am I concerned about other things.

But I come quietly to You,

Just as a little child comes quietly to its mother;

My soul is like a quiet baby before You.

May Your children put their hope in You,

Both now and forever.

Amen

*A song of degrees of David.

PSALM 132

*A Prayer For the Messiah To Come**

Lord, I remember the passion of David;

Who in spite of all his afflictions

He made a vow to You, O Lord;

Promising that he would not enter Your tent,

Nor would he rest in his bed;

Nor would he close his eyes in sleep,
Until he found a place for You, O Lord;
   And that he built a house for You to dwell in.
I have heard about this vow in Ephratah,
   It was repeated in the woods and fields.
That we must come to Your tabernacle,
   And we must worship at Your feet.

Arise, O Lord, from Your rest;
   Let the Ark of Your presence shine.
Let the priest's clothes reflect Your salvation,
   Let Thy saints shout for joy.
For David's sake don't turn away,
   Shine Your face on Your anointed.
You have made a promise to David
   That the fruit of his loins
     Will sit on his throne.
That if his children will obey Your commandments
   That you will teach them,
     They also will sit on David's throne.
For You, Lord, have chosen Zion
   To be the place of Your habitation.
This is where You will rest in eternity;
   This is where You want to live.

You have abundantly blessed this land,
   You have given bread to the poor.
You will spread salvation through the priest,
   And Your people will shout for joy.
You will once again raise up one from David's line,
   The Messiah will hold forth the light!

Your enemies will be humiliated,
  But the Messiah will be crowned in prosperity.

                                        Amen

*A song of degrees.

PSALM 133
*A Prayer For Unity Among Believers**

Lord, I know it is good for Your people
  To live together in unity.
It is like the oil that is anointed
  On the head of Your servants.
Even that trickled down Aaron's beard,
  And dripped on his skirts.
It is like the dew on Mount Hermon,
  And like the dew on all the mountains of Zion.
Because in unity You direct Your blessings,
  Even life forevermore.

                                        Amen

*A song of degrees of David.

PSALM 134
*A Prayer To Bless The Lord**

Lord, I bless You with all Your servants
  Who stand in Your house to bless You.
They lift up their hands in the sanctuary,
  They bless You, Most Holy Lord.
Lord, You who made Heaven and earth;
  You will bless them from Your home in Zion.

                                        Amen

*A song of degrees.

PSALM 135

A Prayer Of Praise That Surveys All God Has Done For His People

Lord, I praise You;
   I join with all Your servants to praise Your name.
With all those who stand in Your house,
   I praise You.
With all those who stand in Your courts,
   I praise You.
I praise You, Lord, for You are good;
   It is pleasant to sing praises to You.

Lord, You chose Jacob for Yourself;
   You chose Israel as Your peculiar treasure.
I know that You, Lord, are great;
   That You, Lord, are above all gods.
You created what You wanted in the heavens,
   The same in the earth and in the sea.
You created all the fog and the mist,
   You created the lightning with the rain;
   You brought us wind and the storm.

You sent the death angel to strike the firstborn,
   Both among people and animals in Egypt.
You sent miracles and signs to Egypt,
   Both upon Pharaoh and his servants.
You smote the great nations on earth,
   And killed their mighty kings.
This included Sihon king of the Amorites,
   Plus Og, king of Bashan, and the other nations.

You gave their land to Your people,

    To Israel for an everlasting heritage.

Your name will continue forever,

    People will remember You throughout generations.

But You will judge Your people when they sin,

    And forgive them when they repent.

The idols of the heathen are made of silver and gold,

    They are the creation of man's hands.

Idols have mouths, but they do not speak;

    They have eyes, but they do not see.

Idols have ears, but they do not hear;

    Neither is there any breath in them.

Those who create the idols are like them;

    Those who worship them are also like them.

But I join with all Israel to bless You;

    I bless You, Lord, with the priests.

I bless You, Lord, who comes to Zion;

    I praise You, Lord, who dwells in Jerusalem.

                      Amen

PSALM 136

A Prayer Of Thanksgiving
For God's Provision In The Past

Lord, I give thanks to You;

    For You are good,

    For Your mercy endures forever.

I give thanks to You, the God over false gods;

    For Your mercy endures forever.

I give thanks to You, the Lord over lords;

> For Your mercy endures forever.

You alone can do great miracles,

> For Your mercy endures forever.

You have made the heavens,

> For Your mercy endures forever.

You stretched out the earth and the seas,

> For Your mercy endures forever.

You created the sun and stars,

> For Your mercy endures forever.

You made the sun to rule our days,

> For Your mercy endures forever.

You made the moon and stars to rule our night,

> For Your mercy endures forever.

You sent the death angel on the firstborn of Egypt,

> For Your mercy endures forever.

You brought Israel out of Egypt,

> For Your mercy endures forever.

You stretched out Your strong arm against the gods of Egypt,

> For Your mercy endures forever.

You divided the Red Sea,

> For Your mercy endures forever.

You brought Israel through on dry land,

> For Your mercy endures forever.

You drowned Pharaoh and his armies in the Red Sea,

> For Your mercy endures forever.

You led Your people through the wilderness,

> For Your mercy endures forever.

You defeated great kings who oppose Israel,

> For Your mercy endures forever.

You executed famous kings,

For Your mercy endures forever.

Sihon, King of the Amorites, was eliminated;

For Your mercy endures forever.

Also Og, King of Bashan, was eliminated;

For Your mercy endures forever.

You gave their land to Your people,

For Your mercy endures forever.

Now the land is the heritage of Israel,

For Your mercy endures forever.

You remember us in our weakness,

For Your mercy endures forever.

You redeemed us from our enemies,

For Your mercy endures forever.

You give everyone food to eat,

For Your mercy endures forever.

I give thanks to You, the God of Heaven;

For Your mercy endures forever.

Amen

PSALM 137

A Prayer To Remember God

Your people sat by the rivers of Babylon,

And wept when they remembered Zion.

They refused to sing joyfully,

Hanging their harps on willow trees.

Their captors demanded that they sing;

Those who imprisoned them wanted entertainment,

Asking, "Sing us a song of Zion."

Your people couldn't sing,

   While being held captive in a strange land.

Your people said they couldn't forget Jerusalem,

   Just as their right hand couldn't forget its movement.

Your people said their tongue would stick in their mouth,

   If we do not remember You, O Lord.

O Lord, don't forget what Edom did to Your people;

   When Jerusalem was being attacked.

Edom was yelling for the city to be destroyed,

   And its foundation to be destroyed.

O Lord, I know You will destroy Babylon;

   Someone will be happy to do it.

They will enjoy destroying the children of Babylon,

   Just as Babylon destroyed Your children.

                                        Amen

PSALM 138

*A Prayer For God's Deliverance In Trouble**

O Lord, I offer praise to You;

   With all my heart.

I sing praise to You,

   And not to idols.

I will worship You in the Temple,

   And praise You for Your love and faithfulness;

   Because You exalted Your name and kept Your Word.

When I called to You in trouble,

   You answered by encouraging me with Your strength.

All the rulers of the earth shall praise You,

When they hear the words You speak.
They shall sing about Your ways,
 And Your glory shall be great.
Even though You are high and lofty,
 You look kindly to the lowly;
 But You know those who are proud in heart.

When I have a lot of trouble,
 You help me through it.
You stretch out Your hand against my enemies,
 Your right hand shall deliver me.
You will fulfill Your plan for my life,
 Your love endures forever;
 Don't quit protecting me.

        Amen

*A Psalm of David.

PSALM 139

A Prayer Of Thanksgiving
*For God's Oversight Of Your Life**

Lord, You have searched me;
 And You know me thoroughly.
You know when I sit and when I rise,
 You understand my thoughts from afar.
You know my journeys and my rest,
 You are familiar with everywhere I go.

Before my tongue speaks a word,
 O Lord, You know what I'm going to say.
You are all about me, in front and behind;

And You have laid Your hand on me.
Being known by You is a wonderful thing,
    You have greater knowledge than anyone.

It is impossible to escape from Your Spirit,
    I can never get away from Your presence.
If I could go to Heaven, You are there;
    If I make my bed in hell, you are there.
If I could fly away on the wings of a new day,
    And fly across the sea;

Even there I would find Your hand guiding me,
    And Your right hand holding me.
If I say that the darkness will surely hide me,
    Even the night covers everything about me.
But I cannot hide from You in the darkness,
    Because the night shines like the day to You;
    Both darkness and light are the same to You.

You made the inner parts of my body,
    You created me in my mother's womb.
I praise You for reverently and wonderfully forming me,
    I recognize Your marvelous creative works.
You saw me being conceived in the protection of the womb,
    And I came together under Your watch care.

All the days of my life were preordained for me,
    You wrote them in a book before they happened.
O God, Your thoughts about me are precious;
    I can't begin to number the times You think about me.
If I could count all of them,
    Your thoughts of me are more than the grains of the sand.

When I wake each morning,
    You are still right beside me.

If only You would destroy the wicked,
    And get rid of all who are trying to kill me.
My enemies blaspheme You,
    They misquote You and take Your name in vain.
Lord, I hate those who hate You;
    And will have nothing to do with those who oppose You.
Yes, Lord, I hate Your enemies as I should;
    For Your enemies are my enemies.

Search me, O God, to know the intent of my heart;
    Try me to know my thoughts.
Point out any wicked inclination in me,
    And lead me in the way of eternal life.

                                        Amen

PSALM 140

*A Prayer To Punish Those Who Attack The Godly**

O Lord, deliver me from evil people;
    Protect me from those who would hurt me.
They think up evil plans in their heart,
    They want to fight me every day.
They sharpen their tongue like a serpent,
    Their words against me are poison. Selah!
Deliver me from the hands of the wicked,
    Protect me from violent people
    Who plan to destroy me.
They arrogantly set a trap for me,

They plan to trip me up
And catch me in their deceit. Selah!

O Lord, You are my God;
Hear my cry to You for help.
O Lord, You are the strength of my salvation;
Protect me in the heat of battle.

Do not let the wicked do what they desire,
Don't let them become proud before You. Selah!
Let my enemies be destroyed,
With the destruction they plan for me.
May burning coals be thrown upon them,
And throw them into the pit never to escape.
Don't let liars prosper on this earth,
May they be hunted down and destroyed.

I know You will do the right thing to the poor,
And protect the rights of the needy.
Then the godly will praise Your name,
And they will live in Your presence forever.

Amen

*A Psalm of David.

PSALM 141

A Prayer For Deliverance From Evil People

O Lord, I cry out to You;
I need You now,
Please listen when I call You.
Let my prayers be the first thing you hear,

And my lifted hands be the first thing that pleases You.
Guard the words that I say,
   And keep my mouth from speaking.
Don't let me lust for evil,
   Nor get involved in wicked acts;
   Nor satisfy myself with transgressors.
Let godly people remind me when I stray,
   And let them rebuke me when I'm stubborn;
   And make me listen to them.

So I will pray constantly
   Against evil and those who do it.
When rebellious people fall,
   The sinners will understand why I live godly.
They will say that as the farmer breaks rocks,
   Even in death our bones are broken and scattered.

But, O Lord, I look to You for help;
   You are my refuge, do not let me die.
Don't let me walk into the trap of my enemy,
   Nor get caught by those who do evil.
Let the wicked fall into their own trap,
   While I walk by safely.

                              Amen

PSALM 142

A Prayer For Deliverance From Trouble

O Lord, I cried out loudly to You;
   Listen when I ask for help.
I poured out my troubles to You

And told You all my difficulties.

When my spirit is about to faint,

    You alone know what I should do.

Everywhere I go in life

    My enemy lays a trap for me.

I look on my right hand for help,

    But there was no one who cares.

I cried out to You, O Lord;

    In this land of the living,

    You are the only One who will protect me.

Listen to my cry,

    For I am discouraged.

Deliver me from my persecutions,

    For they are too strong for me.

Deliver me from my prison,

    So I may praise You.

Then the godly will gather around me,

    As You show me Your goodness.

Amen

*A Psalm of instruction by David; a prayer when he was in the cave.

PSALM 143

*A Prayer For Deliverance From Your Enemies**

O Lord, listen to my prayer;

    Answer me because You are righteous and faithful.

Do not judge my failures,

    Because no one is perfect compared to You.

My enemy is chasing me,

   He has knocked me to the ground;

   I hide in darkness like a dead person.

My spirit is crushed,

   And I have no hope in my heart.

I remember the good old days,

   I think about Your works;

   And I meditate on what You did for me.

Again I stretch out my hands to You,

   I need You, as parched ground thirsts for water. Selah!

Answer me quickly, O Lord;

   For I am discouraged.

Don't hide Your face from me,

   Or I might as well be dead.

In the morning, remind me of Your faithfulness;

   Because I am trusting You.

Show me how to live a godly life,

   Because that's my heart's desire.

Save me from my enemies, O Lord;

   Because I hide in You.

Teach me to do Your will,

   Because You are my God.

Lead me into Your perfect plan for my life,

   Because You are good.

Deliver me from trouble,

   Because You are righteous.

Protect me from now on,

    For Your name's sake.

Cut off all my enemies,

    Destroy them;

For I am Your servant.

Amen

*A Psalm of David.

PSALM 144

*A Prayer For Protection And Prosperity**

Lord, I praise You for being my rock;

    Because You give me strength,

    And You give me skill.

Lord, You are good and You are strong;

    You protect me and You deliver me.

I take refuge in Your protection,

    You defeat the enemies who fight me.

O Lord, what is a mortal person

    That You will be concerned for him,

    Or the Son of Man that You think of him?

A person is like a breath,

    And his days like a passing shadow.

Split Heaven wide open and come to earth,

    Touch the mountains so they smoke.

Strike the enemy with lightning,

    Destroy those who oppose You.

Reach down Your hand from Heaven,

To rid me from dangerous floods;

And from the hands of my enemy,

Who lies about me;

And constantly deceives me.

I sing a new song to You, O God;

On musical instruments I will praise You.

For You give victory to Your leaders,

You delivered Your servant David.

Rescue me from the attack of my enemies,

And from the power of my oppressors.

They tell lies on me all the time,

And they plot deceitfully to destroy me.

May my sons prosper in their youth,

And grow like well-nurtured plants.

May my daughters be like beautiful pillars,

That decorate a magnificent palace.

May our barns be filled with every kind of crop,

And may our flocks multiply and grow;

And our work animals carry heavy loads.

May our walls be safe against the enemy,

And may none of us be carried into captivity.

Lord, we will be happy with life like this;

We will be blessed because You are our Lord.

                                        Amen

*A Psalm of David.

PSALM 145

A Prayer To Magnify God
*Because Of His Faithfulness**

O God, I magnify You, O my King;
  I will bless Your name forever.
Every day I will lift up Your name,
  I will praise Your name forever and ever.
Because You are great,
  I will praise Your name greatly;
  I can never fully understand Your greatness.
Each new generation will praise Your works,
  Telling the next generation of Your mighty power.
I will tell them of Your glory and majesty,
  And of Your wonderful acts.
Others will also tell of Your abundant goodness,
  And loudly sing of Your faithfulness.

You are gracious and compassionate,
  Slow to anger and filled with love.
You are good to all people,
  And show Your mercy to all You created.
All Your Creation will praise You, O Lord;
  All Your saints will bless You.
They will tell of Your glorious rule,
  And tell of Your great power.
As a result, all will know of Your mighty acts;
  And the majestic glory of Your rule.
You will rule forever in an everlasting kingdom,
  You will rule from generation to generation.

You help all those who fall,

And lift up all those who are down.

The eyes of all look to You for help,

You supply their needs in due season.

You open Your hand to us,

You satisfy the desires of all people.

You are righteous in everything You do,

And holy in all Your acts.

You are near to those who call upon You,

To those who sincerely seek Your presence.

You satisfy the desires of those who fear You,

You will hear their cry and save them.

You care for all who love You,

But the wicked will You destroy.

I will magnify You, O my Lord;

Let everyone on earth bless Your holy name,

From generation to generation and forever and ever.

Amen

*David's Psalm of praise.

HOW TO PRAY

When You're Really Happy:
The Hallelujah Psalms

The last five Psalms (146—150) are called the Hallelujah Psalms because each begins and ends with the word in Hebrew *Hallelu-JAH*. (The JAH is Jehovah or Lord). Because the entire Book of Psalms is a prayer to God, the last five Psalms are an echo of "Hallelujah" for everything that has been included. Because these last Psalms shout "Hallelujah," then each one begins and ends with a shout of "Hallelujah."

The authorities call Psalm 146 the "Genesis Psalm" because it praises God for creation and the beginning of everything. "You are the Creator of the Heavens, earth and the seas, and You created everything in them" (v. 6, PTP). *Hallelujah, Lord, for giving us the earth and everything in it.*

Psalm 147 is called the "Exodus Psalm" because it praises God for His kindness to Israel in delivering the nation to lead it back to the promised land. "You are rebuilding Jerusalem, and bringing the exiles back to the land" (v. 2, PTP). *Hallelujah, Lord, for deliverance and restoration.*

Psalm 148 is called the "Leviticus Psalm" about God's sanctuary. It tells us to shout Hallelujah because the entire universe is God's dwelling place. "The heavens praise You. The heights praise You" (v. 1, PTP). Yet God's greatest sanctuary is when He dwells in His people. "The children near Your heart, all praise You, O Lord" (v. 14, PTP). *Hallelujah, Lord, for living in the sanctuary of my heart.*

Psalm 149 is called the "Numbers Psalm" reflecting the judgment of God on His people at Kadesh Barnea (Num. 13—15) and their subsequent wandering in the wilderness. God keeps His promises in both blessing and punishment; therefore, shout hallelujah because, "Your saints have felt Your judgment, You have kept Your word when they sinned" (v. 9, PTP). *Hallelujah, Lord, for Your faithfulness.*

Psalm 150 is the "Deuteronomy Psalm" that repeats the praise for everything that has gone before, just as Deuteronomy repeated everything that had happened to Israel. *Hallelujah, Lord, for all You've done. Hallelujah!*

PSALM 146

*A Prayer To Praise God For His Watch Care**

Hallelujah, Lord,
  I praise You from the bottom of my soul.
I praise You with all my life,
  I will praise You, Lord, as long as I live.
I will not put my trust in human leaders,
  Nor will I trust those who cannot help me.
When they die, they are buried;
  At that time they are gone.

I am blessed because I trust in You, O God;
  You are my hope, O Lord, God of Jacob.
You are the Creator of the heavens, earth, and the seas,
  And You created everything in them.
You remain faithful forever,
  You protect those who are oppressed.
You give food to the hungry,
  You set the prisoners free.
You give sight to the blind,
  You lift up the oppressed;
  And You love those who live righteously.

O Lord, You preserve the strangers;
  And watch over the orphans and widows,
  But confuse the way of the wicked.

O Lord, You reign forever and ever;

    You will always be the God of Israel,

    Hallelujah, Lord.

*A Hallelujah Psalm.

PSALM 147

*A Prayer To Praise God For The Blessings Of Life**

Hallelujah, Lord;

    Praising You is exciting and fulfilling.

You are rebuilding Jerusalem

    And bringing the exiles back to the land.

You heal the brokenhearted,

    You bind up the wounds of the hurting.

You know the exact number of stars,

    You call each of them by their name.

You are great, Lord, and have great power;

    Your understanding is infinite.

You encourage the humble,

    But throw the wicked to the ground.

I give thanks to You with singing,

    I sing praise to You with my harp.

You cover Heaven with the clouds,

    You send rain upon the earth;

    You make grass grow upon the mountain.

You provide food for the wild animals,

    And for the young ravens when they call.

You are not impressed by the strength of horses,
   Nor with the legs of a man.
You take pleasure in those who fear You,
   And in those who put their hope in Your mercy.

I join with Jerusalem in praising You,
   I join with Zion in praising You.
For You fortify the protection of the gates,
   You bless those within Your care.
You send peace to Your people,
   You provide the finest food for them.
Your commandments go out to the earth,
   The influence of Your words spreads quickly.
You send the snow to spread over us,
   You scatter the frost on the ground like ashes.
You cover the ground with ice like pebbles,
   You hurl down hail as a man throwing stones.
Then they are melted according to Your plan,
   You send the wind to thaw the ice.

You give Your Word to Jacob,
   You reveal Your laws and principles to Israel.
You have not done this with other nations,
   They do not understand Your laws;
   Hallelujah, Lord.
*A Hallelujah Psalm.

PSALM 148

*A Prayer Of Worship And Praise**

Hallelujah, Lord;
    The heavens praise You,
    The heights praise You.
The angels praise You,
    The hosts praise You.
The sun and moon praise You,
    The stars of light praise You.
The heavens where You live praise You,
    The waters above the heavens praise You.
They all praise Your name, O Lord;
    For You commanded them to be created.
You have set them in an eternal place,
    You have determined they will never pass away.
The earth praises You,
    The great sea creatures in the oceans' depths praise You.

Lightning and hail, snow and clouds,
    And stormy winds obey Your Word.
Mountains and hills, fruit trees and cedars,
    Wild animals and cattle, small animals and birds.
Kings of all people, princes, and all people,
    And all the judges praise Your name.
Young men and young women, old men and children;
    All praise Your name, O Lord.
Your name is exalted,
    Your glory is exalted above the Heaven and earth.
You have raised up a people to praise You,

All Your saints praise You.

The children of Israel near Your heart

All praise You.

Hallelujah, O Lord.

*A Hallelujah Psalm.

PSALM 149

*A Prayer Of Praising The Lord With Singing**

Hallelujah, Lord;

I will sing to You a new song,

I will praise You in the assembly of saints.

May Israel rejoice in You, God, their Creator;

May the children of Zion be glad in Your rule.

May they praise You in dance,

May they sing Your praise with musical instruments.

Because You take pleasure in Your people,

You make the humble beautiful with salvation.

May Your saints rejoice in Your glory,

Let them sing Your praises at night.

May they praise You with their mouth,

And be alert with a sword in their hand

To carry out judgment upon their enemies;

And punishment upon Your foes,

To put their rulers in prison,

And their staff into chains.

All Your saints have legal privileges

To execute judgment according to the law,

Hallelujah, Lord.

*A Hallelujah Psalm.

PSALM 150

*A Prayer Of Praising The Lord In The Assembly**

Hallelujah, Lord;

Praise You in Your sanctuary,

Praise You in Your vast heavens.

I praise You, Lord;

Praise You for Your mighty works,

Praise You for infinite greatness.

I praise You, Lord;

With the blast of trumpets,

With guitars and bass.

I praise You, Lord;

With my whole body,

With the stringed instruments and flutes.

I praise You, Lord;

With the playing of cymbals,

And the echoes of more cymbals.

Everyone joins me in praising You,

Hallelujah, Lord.

Amen and Amen

*A Hallelujah Psalm.

ALSO BY ELMER L. TOWNS

KNOWING GOD THROUGH FASTING

People fast for many reasons…to break an addiction…to seek God for healing…to discover the answer to a lingering problem…and some fast for revival. But the greatest reason to fast is to get to know God intimately and to feed on the Bread of Life.

This book is not an instruction manual on the methods of fasting or on how to pray. Rather, Dr. Elmer Towns describes the spirit of fasting that leads to an intimate knowing of Jesus Christ.

ISBN 0-7684-2069-5

Additional copies of this book and other
book titles from DESTINY IMAGE are
available at your local bookstore.

For a bookstore near you, call 1-800-722-6774

Send a request for a catalog to:

Destiny Image® Publishers, Inc.
P.O. Box 310
Shippensburg, PA 17257-0310

"Speaking to the Purposes of God for This
Generation and for the Generations to Come"

For a complete list of our titles,
visit us at www.destinyimage.com